Broken

Into

Brilliance

Volume II

A collection of stories from beautiful, brilliant, courageous, and determined women

Published by Write It Away Publishing Co & Shamay Speaks

www.WriteItAwayPublishing.com

www.ShamaySpeaks.com

Book cover designed by Shauny B with KnockSmith Productions www.knocksmithmagazine.com

Printed in the United States of America

ISBN: 978-0-9966729-5-5

Professionally edited by Dayna Plummer (daynariffic) with Fiverr.com

Dedication:

I dedicate this book to all the women who have stepped out of their comfort zone and taken a chance by following their dreams. I also dedicate this book to the single mothers out there who never give up on their goals. I thank all the women who believed in me to lead them during their journey to authorship. I truly appreciate every courageous woman that has allowed me to coach and assist them in accomplishing their goals and sharing their story. **This is just the beginning, ladies.**

Broken Into Brilliance is a collection of short stories from powerful, brilliant, courageous, and determined women who are ready to spread their message by sharing their stories. This book features amazing women from different walks of life, who have gained strength and wisdom from their past while learning to move forward. The book's visionary, Tanicia "Shamay Speaks" Currie, believes that God has the power to show us that through times when you may have felt broken, there's beauty in coming out of that broken place or overcoming those broken feelings. Being able to break through the rough times or circumstances in life is what plays a role in your brilliance as you step out into your purpose. We all have a story that can provide someone with insight, inspiration, and motivation. Being a five time author herself,

Tanicia believes that sharing your story can be the first step to healing and overcoming your past experiences, as she feels her first published book served as her therapy process. Always have faith in knowing you can still be brilliant and resilient despite the cards life has dealt you. Be encouraged!

Do you have a book that is finished and you want it published without doing all the research and work to self-publish?

Let Write It Away Publishing help you!

Book Compilation Visionary and Publisher

Tanicia "Shamay Speaks" Currie

Mother~Author~Publisher~Event Planner/Host~Entrepreneur

925-421-0221

Shamayspeaks@gmail.com

www.ShamaySpeaks.com

www.WriteItAwayPublishing.com

Table of Contents

Foreword

By Monique McCoy

It's not easy to walk in our shoes! That is the case for every writer, who since birth, has always looked at the world a little differently than most people. Our *"who"* always leads to a *what, where, when, and why*. But, the question is how? How is it that one can go through unspeakable things and have the courage to tell it?

In my early 20's I stumbled across a different type of book than the previous books I'd read. It was called a memoir. This was the first time that the character was a real person, and unlike an autobiography, the theme was centered around life-changing events that often lead to a crossroads. That's when I realized that we all have a story, and sometimes it takes someone else to share their story before you can build the courage to tell yours!

Tanicia and I exchanged smiles on a summer afternoon in 2015. I was picking my sons up from their summer program. Almost a year later, through the divine connection of social media, I purchased a ticket to attend her book launch for *"Breaking Through Barriers."* Tanicia, a 3x author at the time, had found healing through sharing her stories and was now giving other women in the community a voice through her book compilations. Each chapter was like a "mini memoir" as these ladies told stories of love, pain and survival. It reminded me that we are much more alike than different. A few months later I was invited to her annual Women's Encouragement Brunch titled "Deep Within Your Soul", where she brought countless numbers of women under the same roof to discuss their deepest thoughts and experiences. The following year I would make my debut in *Breaking Through Barriers Volume 2* and become one of the 35 women she has helped "write it away" and become published authors!

The funny thing is when we first met, for a while I had a feeling as if I had seen her before. I just couldn't figure it out. Was it in the grocery store or at the gas station? Then one day a light bulb went off! The teacher from the summer program! I immediately texted her and we laughed about how small the world is. I am so glad that we met. It seems that Tanicia's theme in life is always centered around uplifting and helping other people. Each book brings more healing and freedom to its authors. She has the gift of seeing greatness in others that they can't see in themselves, helping them get out of their own way. That was surely the case for me.

"Broken Into Brilliance Volume 2" is sure to be yet another stepping stone that leads to the path of freedom and success. Thank God that everything that breaks isn't unfixable, and every story doesn't have a bad end. In this sequel, you will possibly see yourself. It may even jog your memory and dig

up old hurts that you have buried. Nonetheless, it will inspire and encourage you! Mission accomplished!

Monique McCoy

Author~ Writer~ Motivational~ Speaker

Email: itzmorning007@gmail.com

Follow me on Facebook @ Monique McCoy

Instagram @moeministry

PITTSBURG NEWS

Area director releases film

Halloween flick "Jack Lantern" shot partially in East County, features local residents.

FRIDAY, NOVEMBER 3, 2017   SERVING THE COMMUNITIES OF EAST CONTRA COSTA COUNTY SINCE 1904

Inside

PAGE 6

Brentwood church encourages area residents to drop off gifts for Operation Christmas Child

PAGE 9

Library Lines: Antioch Library's permanent manager to take hold of the reins on Monday.

PAGE 3

Officials at Antioch schools OK spending up to $75K on PR.

ONLINE:

Facebook.com/ PittsburgNews

Index

SURVIVING AND THRIVING

'The only failures are quitters'

Pittsburg single mom has undergone four heart surgeries, been part of just as many books. Page 3

Tanicia Shamay Currie appears Oct. 24 with daughter Laniyah Carter, 4, in front of their Pittsburg home. Born with a heart condition, Currie has had four open-heart surgeries, but despite her life's challenges, she was the first in her immediate family to finish college and is now working on her fifth book.

Book Compilation Visionary & Publisher

Tanicia "Shamay Speaks" Currie

Mother~Author~Publisher~Event Planner/Host~Entrepreneur

925-421-0221

Shamayspeaks@gmail.com

www.WriteItAwayPublishing.com

Introduction

I will start with these statements, "No one is exempt from misfortunes," and "Why me?" Life can take so many detours and these detours can leave you with so many questions.

Today is April 15th, 2018 and I should be writing the intro for this amazing book, but my spirit has been all over the place as my mind has been. I decided that being transparent is what I needed to do. I went to church today as I do every Sunday; I feel church starts off my week the right way. I had someone say to me this week, "The true life challenges seems to have started AFTER I got saved." I thought to myself, ya know what, that is true for me. Truth be told, I have had a lot success and blessings this past year, but behind the scenes my life has been "cloudy," if that is the best word to use. Some may think here is this amazing woman who has been a blessing to so many, this woman who has been in the newspaper 2 times in 3 months, this woman who came through her 3rd open heart surgery, this woman who inspires so many, and annually gives back to her community, but that same woman has been struggling behind the scenes. Many think that having many blessings and success translates into she/he must "have it all together," but that's not it. When I sat down to write this, I didn't think I would be as transparent as I am being right now. At this point I am mentally struggling, and

Introduction

I have decided to seek therapy. There have been events in my life over the last 14 months that have changed the trajectory of my life, but I press forward through the storm, tears, highs and lows. You see, in September 2017, I had my 4th heart surgery but 3rd open-heart surgery. Prior to getting the news that I needed to have another open-heart surgery approximately 10 years sooner than expected, I was having the worst year ever. Worst can be defined simply by how one views life and unfortunate situations. My uncle Walter always says "Better than some and worse than others" when asked how he's doing. That answer/statement is true for each of us. I'm sure someone had a worse year than me and my problems that seem big to me may seem small to others. Because of who I am and the perception some have of me, I feel like many feel that my life is issue free, but there we go back to that great word called "perception." Perception is always in the eye of the beholder.

Now those who follow me on social media may think to themselves how could her year have been that bad when she's had a good amount of success? Looks can be deceiving and none of us will ever be exempt from misfortune.

I attend church every Sunday, but after these past 14 months I have to constantly ask myself if I trust the process? God's process and plan for my life, the trajectory of my life. After 3 years of pretty consistent greatness and blessings, I am now battling my success and demons at the same time. I am struggling to figure out how I can pick up the pieces of the storms I have been experiencing this year or so. I struggle, wondering and praying about what direction God is sending me, especially with the storms I've been experiencing. If only there was glue we could buy at our local Wal-Mart to glue the broken pieces of our lives back together. If we could buy some life glue at Wal-Mart, they would have a line out the door and around the corner.

Putting the pieces back together while continuing to strive for greatness is absolutely not easy, however it is possible. We all have to get through issues the best way we know how, because many of us were not necessarily taught to manage life issues and struggles effectively; at times we need guidance. Sometimes your best friend, your mom or dad, or your family are not the ones you want to help you deal with issues. I advocate for counseling/therapy because you have a fresh slate with this skilled person versus asking for help from family or friends who know everything about you or may not have the tools and guidance you need. I feel at times therapy/counseling can help you gain the most clarity. With that being said, I decided to seek counseling for some issues I am experiencing as I have done a couple times in the past. As strong as I am, I needed the guidance from someone who can help me, like from a fresh pairs of lenses or a fresh perception.

Life has been a rollercoaster but year after year, struggle after struggle, I understand more and more just how important keeping my peace is. Whether you seek counseling or church for help/guidance, your peace is what helps you work through issues. I also understand how important it is to create healthy habits, and this includes healthy emotional habits. Whether it takes 21 days or 1 year, we must make it a point to work at it daily, weekly, monthly, etc., until we see a measurable difference/change where we are able to measure our personal growth. I strongly feel nothing changes, especially eternally or spiritually, until healthy habits are created. Going through the process of creating healthy habits requires plenty of self-talk and self-reflection.

I was watching a TEDx speech where a speaker mentioned something called "white time." That's the time when you have no time for anything or anyone but you, whether it's an hour or 30 minutes. I feel it's so extremely important to love YOU because YOU are the one who controls your peace, which translates into how you deal with what life throws at you. We have to work at finding that true inner-peace/freedom. That whole making lemons into lemonade saying is totally true, but I think that it all depends on how tuned-in you are with yourself.

Introduction

I once made a YouTube video called "Undo and Renew," where I spoke about the process of having to undo things but mainly bad habits and the way we speak combined with moving forward in life. Undo is peeling back the layers of issues you may need to acknowledge, address, and move forward from. Layers are things/life situations that hold you back, and these things can be in your control or out of your control. Layers can also be when you need to grieve the loss of your connections/emotional attachments to negative things, feelings, and of course people.

When consistently working towards undoing and renewing, you are able to start to slowly find that inner-peace leading to freedom. That word "freedom" encompasses a few meanings; it just depends on the context you choose to use it in. If you have no inner-peace, I personally don't believe that you can truly gain freedom. It doesn't even matter if you cry for a day as long as you continue move forward, baby steps are included. Even crying helps cleanse the soul, and many times it is truly necessary. With everything I've been through in my life and everything I've come through, I still see room for improvement daily. We must make a solid effort to move forward no matter what. I am still working on peeling back the layers and working on me daily, because if I don't, this "cloudy mind" will overtake me. Working at peeling back those layers as you move forward is where accountability can be most uncomfortable in your growth season. I know this all sounds like "easier said than done," but it's possible when you are consistent, little by little. Every true change that is worthwhile is like that old saying: Nothing good comes easy.

Sometimes it's okay for many of us to understand that it is 100% okay to not be okay, if that makes sense. The reality is none of us have it completely together 100% of the time. We all have flaws and weaknesses; it's truly a matter of how you choose to deal with them. Life is guaranteed to have storms and highlights, but even storms settle, which allows you to keep moving. I really had a hard time completing this introduction, which is something that hasn't happened my last 5 books, but I'm pushing forward through the storms. It is possible to work through the storms, and I can testify the blessings gained from moving forward can be life changing. I say that because I can testify to that, because through my current storms, I was still able to continue to be the best mother I can be, I published books, hosted events, gave back, successfully survived my 3rd open heart surgery, and more. You can accomplish goals; it is possible even if you are forced to move through the storms in the midst of achieving them. I want this intro and this book to bless you, and for you to see there are blessings in storms.

Lastly, At church one Sunday, my pastor Shaun Nepstad cited a scripture that stood out to me: The Call of Abram **12** The

Introduction

LORD had said to Abram, *"Leave your native country, your relatives, and your father's family, and go to the land that I will show you. ²I will make you into a great nation. I will bless you and make you famous, and you will be a blessing to others"* Genesis 12:1-3 New Living Translation (NLT). This scripture spoke to me, and what I took away from this is that we have to leave our comfort zone in order to find success, but we must also trust God and the process. It also speaks to how you can bless others, which is exactly part of this amazing book's goal. These remarkable women stepped out to share their stories to bless others within their journey. They share their stories as part of the healing process for themselves as well as be a blessing to others in the world with their message that you can transition from Broken Into Brilliance.

Look out for my solo book titled *"Why Me, But Why Not Me,"* to fully understand where my life was at this point.

"Speak out for those who cannot speak." Proverbs 31:8 NIV

Broken to Resilient

"She Overcame & Conquered"

By

Jocelyn Ja'Net Willis

Sisters with Stories Founder C.E.O~Media
Host~Author~Makeup Artist

Email: sisterswithstories@gmail.com

Mailing Address P.O. Box 51013 Fort Worth, TX 76105

(405) 771-0837

On the third month and twenty - eighth day of nineteen seventy-nine, I began my journey. Not only was I born to a single mother and to a married man, my birth father was married when I was conceived. I was extremely impatient and made my arrival to let the world know that I was here. Who was this infant who mastered her way despite all that was against her? She rested peacefully in her rectangular glassed incubator with tubes in her head. There was something so uniquely different about this blessed infant. She hurried her way to earth weighing only two pounds. Deep down, she had enough faith to conquer all that would come against her. This baby girl was ready and willing to show every adversary that resilience comes from within. Jocelyn Ja'Net was born two months early! The number two had a significant place in her life. I believe it meant she would endure to witness a double portion. Her mother unfortunately miscarried once and later lost another baby prior to her birth.

Despite her siblings' demise, Jocelyn courageously conquered and surfaced to the land of the living. I was the chosen vessel who was predestined to overcome and conquer. I'm amazed that even as a tiny infant I was broken. Not only was my body not fully developed but my destiny was being challenged. Not only was I born to a single mother but also to an attached man. As I fought to gain weight I was preparing to make my exit out of the hospital. I never knew what was ahead of me. I was diagnosed with mitral valve prolapse which consists of a heart murmur. I loved seeing my heartbeat on the screen as the wires were attached to my body. I never knew that this condition would rob me of doing things that I loved. Basketball and gymnastics were out for me. I was disappointed, but I tried to enjoy my childhood.

My life was never the definition of perfection; it was far from it. I would watch this estranged man come in and out of my home. I was told he was my father, but his actions didn't measure up. He made his presence known by giving me a dollar as he would then make his way to my mother. This was the beginning of how I viewed my worth. I was very inquisitive and wondered why he didn't stay long enough to spend time with me. There you have it: From the seeds sown, brokenness was blossoming from the internal. I never realized what a single mother was until I saw my mother crying, begging for support from my father. She finally got court ordered help which wasn't very much.

I remember the girl who sat on the porch in Elizabeth Court on the Southside of Fort Worth. I sure do remember her; she had a best buddy named Latrice who shared her granny named Callie. My grandmother lived far away in Munday, Texas so I didn't see her much, but I loved it when she sent me brownies through the mail. I rode my Smurfette big wheel up and down the apartment complex. As soon as I heard the ice cream truck, Callie met Latrice and I to give us quarters. My bony little knees would always knock as if someone was going to answer a door. Laugh out loud! I was a fun-loving kid who would sit and watch my big brother play football out in the field. But wait, what happened? I didn't stay long in this place that I adored. It was a place where I embodied being a kid.

I went to a place of no return, but little did I know she was STILL THERE! My body was forced to engage in adult behavior. Let me stop, I was RAPED by a grown ass man. I was raped repeatedly in my very own home. He was a Baton Rouge ordained minister who captivated my mother's heart. He was a sheep in wolf's clothing pretending to be a genuine man of God. He had a plan to disguise himself as a man of God and go forth with his plan.

I was sexually assaulted the first time in my apartment when my mother left us with him. I endured five years of this abuse due to the threat he made of killing my mother and brother. I wanted to protect them. I was taken from the essence of my very own childhood. My life was in the hands of this man daily. Ironically, I was also in the hands of the most high God. In my little mind I wondered why, and I knew this wasn't ok. One morning I thought I could protect myself by hiding in the back of my mother's car, but I made a noise and she made me go back in the house. Well at least I tried! My six year old self had to build up enough courage to tell my best friend. She couldn't hold water, meaning she couldn't keep a secret. Latrice spoke up for me and no one listened. Then I found out that we were moving to the West Coast. Before we made it to California we stopped and stayed in motels overnight. This was another opportunity for this man to sexually assault me again. I'd wash myself and get dressed and we'd be on our way. We made it to Pittsburg, California and I wasn't happy about the move. My brother and I were furious that our mother decided to marry this man.

We ended up staying in El Pueblo where I met our new roommates. A nice lady allowed us to room at her place. We spent so much time together and we became an instant family. I remember hanging with my cousins and I felt like a kid again. If we weren't playing outside I was running up and down the street. I'd always find myself coming back to the house with a scraped knee. The first day of school came around and I thought it had a weird name. I was enrolled at Heights and later ended up at Village Elementary. My school was huge and I didn't want to leave it once the bell rang for dismissal. My teacher was the greatest; his name was Mr.

Miller and he loved his students. I felt safe when I was in his classroom. I met some really cool friends, too.

Phylethia, Tamara, Nefertari, and I would kill it with the double Dutch. When you think back can you remember a bully you had at your school? Well let me say my bully was huge; she looked like she was enrolled in Pittsburg High. Boy oh boy was I afraid when I saw her coming my way. It wasn't until I told my cousin Edward and he was very seriously considering taking her down. Laugh out loud, he didn't play!! The next day while playing on the playground I saw my cousin pull up on his bike. I ran to the gate to see what he wanted. I knew it; he was there on bully patrol!! He was teaching me that it wasn't ok to be abused in any kind of way. We have to identify the beacons of light in our lives that usher us towards resilience. We never knew how strong our bond would grow.

My family and I later moved away from our extended family's home and got our own place. Our new place was huge, or at least I thought it was. I met some great friends while living there. I met Maria and later her little sister named Shamayia. We became the best of friends. We played for hours together nearly each day. The street lights would come on and we had to depart. It was sad for me, though not just because our play time was over.

Joy would come in the morning as I woke up to stare at my New Edition, The Boys & Michael Jackson posters on my wall. I just knew I'd marry Hakim or Michael Bivins for sure. Music was my outlet to jam to the beat and get lost in the lyrics. My little voice would sing as loud as I could and enjoy simply being a kid. Friday mornings were something special, though! My big brother would comb my hair and drive me to school. My mom had to head to work a bit early and catch the BART train. We'd jump into his powder blue car and he'd blast music, always bumping Too Short. He would drop me off at my school, which was next door to his (Pittsburg High). I'd find myself singing these are the tales the freaky tales. Thank goodness I wasn't aware of what those lyrics meant.

At the end of the day I'd hear the school bell ring and I'd walk over to his high school. I knew exactly who I was looking for and it wasn't my brother. It was these two cuties named Mike and Eric. I would walk down those long hallways and I'd hear someone say hey little Chris. I never found his two friends but my brother sure would find me. When March rolled around it meant it was almost time for my birthday. I always wanted to do it big and I loved having sleepovers. I was a spoiled kid; predators always know how to entice kids. Sadly, my friends were sexually assaulted by my step father. They never told me but I just knew they were. Some years went by and then I was rescued from the hands of this evil man. I was asked to take all my clothes and start packing. We were moving back to Texas. I was devastated! I began to cry because I thought about all my friends I'd leave behind. I had my heart set on going to Central Junior High.

My mother dropped a bomb, saying my brother was staying in California and she would meet me in Texas. I had to say good-bye to my Auntie Eve, and I truly hated leaving her. She was my everything and I hugged her tight each time I was in her presence. She had these hands that would knock someone clear across the country. She didn't play! One day my step dad came to her house and she reached out her arms to shield me. There was no way he was going to take me from her. I saw the fear in his eyes and he quickly bounced! I was amazed at her power and love. He didn't get to take me that day. He wasn't going to brutally rape my body because he was headed to prison. Someone finally stood up and spoke out. All I remember is that he was off to prison and I was preparing to catch my flight. I had to say farewell to my friends and family. I landed at the Dallas airport where my Aunt was waiting to pick me up. I was feeling like I was in a foreign land being back in Texas. I missed my brother so much and I was miserable.

The time had come and I had to get registered for school. I was crying my eyes out because I didn't know anyone. The only thing I could think about was getting home to play with Pebbles. I loved this dog; she was the best little dog and she loved me. My aunt was married and I lived in their home at 1617 Pamela Lane. My uncle had a son and his name was Brandon. I would get so excited when he came over to visit. He was my dude; we got in so much trouble but we had fun. We'd play on his skateboard as Pebbles ran after us down the street. I forgot all about the abuse I endured when we played together. We were the cool kids, as his big brother Bubba would say. The school year went by pretty fast. I was starting high school soon and I wore my cool blue chucks Brandon gave me. It was around this time my mother made her way back and we moved into our new place. We moved to Wood Haven and it wasn't a safe area to live. I mean you could literally go outside and get approached by a dope boy. I was willing and ready to kick it, too. I became familiar with the street life. My friends always knew about the hottest parties. My next encounter with sex was as a teenager.

Things began to escalate and I began drinking and smoking. I was broken, and sex became my new high when I was introduced to this guy named Terry. Hanging with my girls Lele and Jennifer was helping me push my past to the back burner. It was crazy, though, because some nights I'd get these triggers in my mind. I'd remember the sound of my abuser's belt as he would unbuckle it. I would wake up sweating and clutching my pillow. My nights were cold while I dreamt of drowning in my sorrow. I wanted my heart to stop and my breath to be no more. God never answered that desire that circled within my spirit. No one was reaching out to me while I was at my lowest low. I cried out and no one was listening but God. I decided to go back to church in the late nineties. I truly believed that God could help me break free from my pain. I needed an outlet to release my pain and agony. I pleaded with God to let me leave this place, all while going to church. Thank God for his grace.

I was falling into a greater depth of weariness while sorrow strangled my soul. Yet, I still needed another outlet so I picked up my pen and paper. Writing became holistic for me and it lifted me to greater heights. In many ways writing became my fuel to stand despite all that I've endured. Each time I felt lost and alone I'd pick up my pen.

When brokenness collided with resilience it developed my poetry. At the end of each nightmare about my past I'd make my way back to church. I would visit this church called The Chosen Vessel. I was eighteen around the time I started visiting. When the word was taught, it was by this man who was small in stature but the word he preached was powerful. I went back a few times and decided to join the church. It was in God's presence where He would start His plan for my restoration. As I received the word of God my life began to transform. I knew it would be a lifetime process, but I was willing to believe. It was a light unto my feet and a lamp unto my pathway. I was lead to this place called the Women's Center. I met a lady name Lynn Guy who gave me great counsel. It still wasn't enough to get me to that place of wholeness. I later met with Bishop Richard E. Young who told me that God was going to heal me. One night as I was falling to sleep, God confirmed what He had said. I believed God because I knew He was completely able. I trusted him like never before but continued with my writing. I decided to take all of my hurtful writings and put them in a book. I wanted to be loved past my pain and I wanted others to hear my voice. It was my voice that was silenced for so long and I wanted to speak.

I went on to live my life discovering the beauty and strength of me. It was the grace of God that found me. I met a man who reached out to me about sharing my story on his radio show. It didn't happen instantly but he asked me on a few occasions. Gregory simply said when you are ready. I finally had the courage and my story just leaped from my lips. I went from brokenness to resilience by standing on my story and not in it. I give God the glory for freeing me. From down south to the Bay area, God had plans for me. It is my prayer that you will find your very own resilient place.

Jocelyn Ja'Net Willis Biography

Sisters with Stories Founder C.E.O~Media
Host~Author~Makeup Artist

Jocelyn Ja'Net is a two-time author, makeup artist, philanthropist and freelance media host. She has a determination to succeed towards fulfilling every piece of her passion.

From the outside looking in, it looked like her future was bleak. She was born in Fort Worth, Texas. She later moved to Pittsburg, California. As a young girl, Jocelyn endured sexual assault at six years old. She was ten years old when it all came to an end. The abuse led her down a devastating path. However, Jocelyn didn't let this adversity cause her to give up. Instead, she used it to fuel herself for greatness.

Jocelyn is now leading survivors towards freedom. She is the CEO/Founder of Sisters with Stories. They share stories while standing on Revelations 12:11.

Others have started to back her cause too, including Felicia Guimont, Southern Best Catering, Trent Shelton, WFAA reporter Rebecca Lopez, and Jesse Holley. She was featured as a Pat Smith's Second Chance Story, and a 10 Shades of Success Honoree 2017.

Her interviews include: Bishop Richard E. Young, Senior Pastor of The Chosen Vessel Cathedral Church, NFL Hall of Famer Emmitt Smith, Actress Keshia Knight Pulliam, Gospel Artists Kirk & Tammy Franklin, Pastor Dave Hollister, Actress (Bay Area) Brely Evans, Curls Organic Hair Products C.E.O Mahisha Dellinger, Southern Dallas Magazine C.E.O James Thomas, Women Called Moses Founder/President Debra Nixion-Bowles, and Entrepreneur Extraordinaire Anita Hawkins, just to name a few.

She enjoys feeding the homeless in Dallas Fort Worth and serving in the Bay Area Community.

Healing & Forgiveness

Courage to Heal

By

Julie France Bennett

Marseille, France

Wife, Mother, Public Speaker, Certified Victim Advocate, Founder of Women Without Limits, Healthcare Executive, and Philanthropist.

Email: juliebennett813@gmail.com

Healing from current or past pains can be very difficult. I am sure if more people had the tools and support to truly heal, as opposed to putting Band-Aids over their wounds which only provides a temporary solution for potential long term visible scarring, fewer people would live life angry, hurting, bitter, lonely, ashamed, broken, lost, and confused. However, the truth is that healing takes courage. Most often we find that we do not realize how brave and capable we are of healing until the hurt literally damages us, to the point where we may feel beyond repair. For some of us the pains of life have literally saturated through our hearts and minds and hardened the very person we are fighting not to become. Unresolved hurts will keep you in bondage and will not allow you to live a purpose-driven life. Healing from past or even current hurts can be especially difficult when addressing hurts, hang-ups and disappointments of betrayal, deaths, trauma, broken homes, relationships, divorces, infidelities and so forth. I know this first hand because I too was once this very same broken individual. I was the woman most thought had it "all together." Indisputably, I looked good on paper, but inside I was shattered, hiding behind facades. I hid behind my over-achievements, walls of shame, pain, mistrust, and self-hatred. Although I had excelled academically and professionally, I was lost psychologically and emotionally. I was an adult woman trapped by the broken little girl who never had a true opportunity to heal and grieve from significant pains of the past. Pains which mirrored child abuse, child rape, abandonment, rejection and dysfunction. Pain which mirrored witnessing domestic violence, addiction and self-hatred. Pain which mirrored never being able to really experience a happy, loving childhood. Pain which mirrored being a motherless child, never feeling good enough and feeling lost. I was the exact definition of a broken child who transformed into a broken adult; the difference was the way I concealed the pain. I did not cope with the pain by using drugs, alcohol or other visible forms of addiction. However, I chose to cope with the pains of my past by ignoring the triggers, silencing the voices of the many nightmares I experienced, and ignoring the root behind the many angry and emotional outbursts I would often experience. I chose to cope with the pains of the past by not letting people too close, never truly loving others (I mean how could I; after all, I was drowning in a pool of self-hatred which no one knew about). I hid behind fake smiles, unrealistic success, and false pretenses masking who I truly was. Pain held me hostage to ever truly exploring who I was. I had become a successful yet lost and broken woman whose heart was shattered. I lived a life that was unhappy, empty and misdirected. I secretly wished to die, until a diagnosis caused me to have to fight for my life, which ultimately led me to Christ.

I can recall first giving my life to Christ and then beginning on my healing journey He set before me. My life changed suddenly. For the first time ever I felt peace, love, joy and other emotions I had never experienced before. In Christ I had suddenly found true strength, comfort and a freedom I could not explain. Freedom to pray and cry over the hurts of my past which left me broken and bitter, freedom to cry over never being able to know what a mother's love would ever feel like, freedom from self-hatred and insecurities, freedom from nightmares and panic attacks and so much more. In Christ I had finally found my identity, and I was no longer lost and bound to the chains that kept me shackled to pain and confusion. The Bible gave me a roadmap to my healing journey, including learning how to love myself, forgive myself, and understand the capacity of God's love for me, amongst other things. Now I must admit that although I have grown so much in Christ, it was not always easy. You see, although these miracles had transpired in my life, and although I could see and feel the change within me and others could too, I still had questions, and my heart yearned for answers. Satan tried his best to get me back to a place of brokenness and confusion. He did his best to remind me of my "ugly past" and set up situations to mirror past circumstances I had overcome through Christ in order to see my response. Several other life changing situations transpired in my life where the enemy attempted to convince me that God did not care about me.

However, the more I read my word, the more I understood that God is truly a good father who loved me when I could not love myself. See, unlike people, God loves us exactly for who we are because He created us. When I finally understood that, my faith increased and the many questions I once had lessened. Over time I no longer had to ask God "Why me?", because God began showing me other people in the Bible who had endured the same thing I had or even worse, and provided a road of recovery and wholeness during their storm and brokenness. I also received the revelation that Jesus truly understands abuse; He suffered the greatest abuse just for me. He even died just so I could live. As I continued my healing journey I also came to realize that God gives us the hope and tools to truly heal from pains, and I am a living testimony that there is nothing too hard for God. Because of God I am now able to love freely, and have been able to forgive my abusers and others who hurt me that I used to hate. This is all through God's grace and His allowing me to be set free from the bondage that chained me for so many years. In my healing God also revealed to me that He saw my abuse and did not condone it. It was then that I turned my mindset from victim to victor and began on a journey of advocacy and speaking out for those who are not capable of doing so.

Today, I am happily married to the love of my life, and we have a precious baby boy, our miracle baby, which I never imagined possible. My family is proof of how much God truly loves me, and how rewarding the courage to heal can be. I finally understand that healing is a powerful choice which draws forgiveness and grace to ourselves and those who hurt us. Being rooted in Christ has taught me just that. In my continuous journey of healing and seeking peace and joy I, seek happiness in God and not in things or people. In God I have found my true love, joy and peace and healing. I am still here, transformed, redeemed, healed and free!

(Photo provided by Julie Bennett)

Blog Talk Radio:

http://www.blogtalkradio.com/womenwithoutlimitsradio

Facebook Group:

https://www.facebook.com/groups/368945393558409

Julie Bennett Biography

Wife, Mother, Public Speaker, Certified Victim Advocate, Founder of Women Without Limits, Healthcare Executive, and Philanthropist.

Julie Bennett is a devout Christian, wife, mother, victim advocate, public speaker and a successful healthcare executive. Julie was born and raised in Europe and moved to the United States at the age of 18 to study at Fisk University. Julie is trilingual, French being her native language, German her secondary language and English her tertiary language. Despite having gone to school in Germany and then transitioning to American school prior to moving to Nashville, she graduated with a BS in Biology and a master's degree in Clinical Psychology, and is a proud member of Alpha Kappa Alpha.

Julie loves being a wife to her amazing husband and best friend Cedrice L. Bennett, M. Th, and mother to their son and miracle baby Cedrice David Bennett the most. Out of all her accolades, she has been quoted as saying that being a wife and mother has been her best accomplishment to date. She strives to be the best Godly wife and mother God expects her to be, and the wife and mother her husband and son need. She also strives to be the Proverbs 31-woman in all that she does.

Furthermore, she is a passionate victim advocate and loves helping broken people heal; specifically, children and adult survivors of childhood trauma, and victims who have been sexually and or physically abused are her area of expertise. She enjoys helping them gain their voices, and transform themselves from victims to victors through finding hope and healing in Jesus Christ. Her desire to help those who are hurting heal propelled her to launch a non-profit organization, which transitioned from the Healing and Hope Foundation to a current women's group called Women Without Limits. Professionally she enjoys working in the healthcare industry, where she is fervent about cultivating processes for better patient care and healthcare operations one process at a time.

Julie feels blessed to have discovered the freedom to live victoriously through applying God's Word to her life and in turn desires to help others do the same. From her struggles of everyday life, she speaks openly and practically about her experiences so others can apply what she has learned to their lives.

She is an incredible testimony to the dynamic, redeeming work of Jesus Christ. She believes that regardless of a person's background or past mistakes, God has a place for them and can help them on their path to enjoying everyday life.

Broken to Wholeness

"From the Frying Pan Into the Fire"

By

Tracy L. Tate Jones

Business Professional~ Entrepreneur~ Mentor ~ Author

www.tljprofessionalservices.com

(415) 305-5361

Follow me on Facebook and LinkedIn

I am Tracy Tate Jones, born and raised in San Francisco's Bayview District with my maternal great grandmother until the age of 14, upon her passing. I then lived with my maternal grandmother who was lost after the passing of her mother. This left me with no outlet for motherly love and guidance. I practically raised myself from that time and looked for love and acceptance in anything I could find. I made a lot of irresponsible decisions in life and love. One thing that was prevalent in my life was to complete my education and maintain a job. I come from a family of successful individuals so I knew the importance of education and success. Life was not bad, but I did everything at an early age. I was usually first to do or experience everything in high school, good or bad. I started drinking and smoking a lot, but always went to school and work. I completed my high school diploma and had my only child at 19 years old. He is everything to me and through it all, he has been right there.

In 1995, my life changed forever. A couple of years earlier I had met who I thought would be my forever love. We were together for 3 years, a year before my world tragically changed. We were both addicts and moved from place to place with my then 5 year old son. We moved to Oakland after returning from a journey of recovery, only to get caught right back up in addiction. One evening after I completed my homework towards my BA degree, my man "Mister" went out but returned shortly after. I didn't know where he had went and didn't' care. He returned and we went to sleep, only to be awakened by our front door being kicked in by 4-5 goons who rushed into our bedroom. They made my son come into our bedroom and lie on the floor with us as they interrogated us. At this time in my relationship I wanted out, but I was trying to keep it together. I had lost all respect and desire for Mister. If I had $10 to put him on BART that evening, I would have done so. When the goons continued to interrogate us, one of them began to brutally abuse me physically and sexually. Over the course of 5 hours, I was pistol whipped, kicked in my vagina, stomped on my head, a broom stick handle rammed up my body, and a fist and the barrel of a gun rammed up my vagina and rectum. I was being tortured in front of Mister and my son. All they kept saying was "You know what we do to witnesses", so I was scared beyond measure for my life and my child's life. I was also grateful that Mister was there and we were not alone. All I could think was thank God I did not put him on BART. After a couple of hours of being in our home, asking a lot of questions and making threats, they realized that I did not match the description of the female they were looking for, but Mister did match the male. I had a tattoo on my back of the names of me and Mister, which proved who I was. I kept saying "Go get my purse out my car" because I did not have my ID on me. My tattoo saved my life. Little did I know Mister had rented out the car with my purse tucked under the seat.

That was why they were not listening to me say "Look in my car".

After being brutally tortured, I was sexually assaulted multiple times over the course of the remaining 2 hours before they left our unit. During that time, I heard them speaking from our bedroom window to the bedroom window below our top floor unit. They located the female they were looking for in that unit. Apparently, her and Mister were doing Lord knows what while I was at work and messed with the wrong people. All I could think was I don't care if they kill him, but don't hurt my son. I had those thoughts, but remembered "We don't leave witnesses" so I begged for our lives. During the last sexual assault, I thought to myself what do I have to lose if I fight him off, but didn't know how many were still in the house. I wanted to buck him over my back, but felt the cold gun barrel on my lower back just as soon as I had the thought. I began to shake uncontrollably, which I think scared him because he got up. As he continued to watch us and my continuous shaking, he came and put a sheet over my naked body and became concerned. He asked me why I was shaking since he had covered me and I responded "I've never been through anything like this and I'm scared." He said "We not gonna take nothing and you're ok." Who was he to say that to me after raping me multiple times and after the other torture I endured? I just couldn't stop shaking. I could tell he was young, especially when he began to pace the floor, saying "I have a mother and father too." He was panicking big time. At some point I must have blacked out, but then heard Mister say he couldn't hear anyone so we quickly got up, put on clothes and rushed to my cousin's house 10 blocks away. I ducked at every passing car on the street, scared to death.

The worst part of this ordeal is that my son heard every word and every sound, but also saw the face of the person who raped me. My son said he had to pee and I yelled, "Just pee on yourself." The goon told him "Don't pee on yourself little man, stand up and pee, but don't look at me." In doing so, my son saw him in the mirror. He even told the police his name, but gave the wrong description of the person. The name of the person he gave was someone familiar to Mister and me in our addiction. When they asked me about the name, my description didn't match so it was a dead end lead. Many years later I found out that my son told them the correct person's name, but was coerced into providing an inaccurate description out of fear the goon would come back and hurt his mommy again. The one person that we thought we could trust was the one person that got me victimized and lied about it. Needless to say, we broke our lease and moved back to SF. We lost everything we had since our unit didn't have a front door and the neighborhood helped themselves to our belongings.

I was so ashamed and embarrassed by what happened to me and stayed away for several months, even from Mister and my son. They did not know where I was, but knew I was alive. My son was with my aunt who cared for him while I was recovering from my trauma. After a couple of months I went back to work and acted like nothing happened. I drowned the images and fear with work. As more information came out about the traumatizing event, I learned of Mister's wrongdoings that caused the home invasion. Our relationship was already strained from the addiction so learning this was the icing on the cake and that was it for me. Mister was not ready to let me go so he began stalking me, vandalizing my property and even kicked in my door in the middle of the night. This was less than 6 months after the home invasion. I found comfort in an old friend. Mister set him up to be arrested to get him away from me. My old friend had one of his good friends come check on us after hearing of Mister kicking in the door, breaking windows, etc. I was grateful for this friend and saw him as a knight in shining armor. One evening my friend came by to check on us when Mister was visiting our son. Mister stabbed him many times and tried to kill him in a rage. Mister wanted to get rid of any man that was near me. The idea of losing me was not in his plans. My friend had just saved my life and it almost cost him his. I went to check on him to thank him for stepping in to help me through Mister's rage. He was my savior, so I thought. I fell for his Southern charm and heroic efforts. When he healed from the attack, he moved in with me and my son. He was so great to us at first, but soon after his addiction became overbearing too. I went from the frying pan with Mister into the fire with who I thought was my knight.

Over the next six to nine months, I was living in hell. This man became physically and emotionally abusive and often threatened to kill me. After Mister's acts, I believed this man when he said "If I can't have you, no one can". After all, Mister used to imply that too. These were the worst days of my life. I was desperately afraid of losing my life and would say "If you kill me, please take my son too because I am all he has". My family never knew I was being abused as I was afraid and I hid it well. I lost my home, my job, my child to CPS, and my sanity. I even had a nervous breakdown, which I always thought was an excuse, until I lived it. I literally lost everything I had and myself. Drowning my trauma and memories in work and school were no more because I lost them both, right after completing my BA degree. I had to gain the courage and strength to leave the relationship, but how? One day I was talking to his mom and told her he was going to kill me and I was scared. She heard the fear in my voice. In a split moment, I said "I will kill him before he kills me". It was like a light bulb came on and I said it again. That time she heard a difference in my voice and became scared for me and probably her son as well. We were forced to move in with her after we were evicted and left my son to be cared for by his dad's family. During our stay at his mom's house, he would beat me up for nothing and then leave. One day, he beat me up really bad and left as usual. I ran downstairs, gave his mom a hug and told her she would never see me again. I ran out the back door and down the dirt trail as fast as I could to jump on the 29 bus. I rode it to my cousin's house and then drove to get my son and we went to my aunt's house in Oakland. We stayed there for a couple of months before going back to SF. My son went back to his grandmother's house and I lived here and there. I would see my ex in the dark, flicking cigarettes off the roof top of the next building every time I stayed the night with my son. Although it spooked me, I was still in the mindset that I would kill him if he tried to hurt me so I wasn't as scared. Plus I had seen the coward in him when he was confronted by men and would back away like a punk.

Over the next 5 years I lived in a fog; I was homeless and lifeless as I didn't know who this person was in my body. My son was being taken care of so I thought that was good enough. It wasn't until I was told that I couldn't see him anymore that I realized I had truly lost everything. He was all I had, so I had to do something about it. I went to a program that helped me begin my healing process. Not only did I have to face my traumatic events, I also had to overcome the grief and loss of my great grandmother at 14 years old and my mother at 19 years old, not to mention the abandonment issues I had and also passed down to my son. From the time of my assault to the time of my program, I had so much mental trauma that I left him to fend for himself. Through my trials and tribulations, I had to overcome the stereotypes that counseling is for crazy people, they don't know my situation, who are they to tell me how to get over this trauma, what trauma, etc. More importantly, I had to get over the thoughts about why me, how could God allow this to happen to me, it's all my fault, and what about me as well as the embarrassment and shame. Group counseling and individual counseling helped me have a voice to release the shame and embarrassment. Talking about my trauma allowed me to heal and give it to God. The more I told my story, the more power I felt within. I also found solace in my childhood church home, Bethel AME in SF, where I strongly felt my great grandmother's presence. For so long I drowned my sorrows in work and school, but It wasn't until I sat in church on my birthday, also Mother's Day that year, that tears rolled down my face uncontrollably. I had felt alone for so long and in the moment of a Mother's Day song, I felt the presence of my mother and great grandmother's arms around me. Tears flowed for about 20 minutes uncontrolled. All I could do was wipe my tears over and over. From that moment on, I felt the sense of comfort and control. It was at that moment I forgave God for the terrible tragedy I endured and saw the purpose of my life: to encourage others. I am in a space where I am at peace with who I am, what I've been through and my life. I AM A SURVIVOR, with a purpose and voice to encourage others in my life's journey. Live life as if there is no tomorrow. You need to count your Blessings and be a Blessing to others. I've learned to see the blessings in every lesson, experience, obstacle and event that life brings, even those that hurt, as it is a blessing to go from Broken to Wholeness.

Stay tuned for my book titled **Five Years in a Fog** to be released at a later date.

Beat the Streets, Inc.
Young Adult Employment, Vocational & Life Services

Beat the Streets, Inc.

https://www.facebook.com/beatthestreetsinc/

Tracy L. Tate Jones Biography:

Business Professional~ Entrepreneur~ Mentor ~ Author

Tracy L. Tate Jones, a mother, grandmother, wife, and CEO, is a native of SF's Bayview District. Having a passion and desire to help the youth in her community and beyond, she started her nonprofit, Beat the Streets, Inc., in Pittsburg, CA in 2005 to provide resources for education, employment and life skills to young adults. It was founded to stop the youth from hanging out around her home. Welcoming them into her home allowed them to develop a bond that would lead to the services offered today in Antioch, CA.

Her educational background includes receiving an AA Degree from Heald Business College, a BA & MBA in Business with emphasis on Accounting & Public Administration from the University of Phoenix, and a master's certificate in Accounting from Keller Graduate School.

Aside from her philanthropic passions, Tracy is also the CEO of TLJ Professional Services, Inc., an accounting professional of over 30years, and provides administrative, bookkeeping, and tax preparation for individual and small businesses. Tracy is also a life and health insurance provider licensed in CA, NV, TX, IL, adding GA.

Tracy is motivated to share her story to encourage other women to LIVE life fully. The trials she endured are a true testimony of courage, endurance, and a never ending will to live. Tracy counts her blessings to be a blessing to others.

The Fight

By

Marilyn A. Waters

Author

San Leandro, Ca

I am a fighter. Fighting is a part of my genetic makeup. I had to fight for my life upon entering the world, although I would learn much later in life that the battle did not belong to me. I had a womb mate. I have no recollection of the nine month incarceration we shared in our mother's womb, however I was told about how I almost died upon entering the world and of the complications of a premature birth. Fighting to live has been the theme of my life.

My childhood was great! Adolescence was trying; somewhere along the way I decided to jump start my adult life by graduating from high school a year earlier than scheduled. My future was bright. I had a great job, and I loved the Lord with all my heart, mind, soul and strength. I was excited to have a job with benefits. I met a woman who loved the Lord and was excited for me to meet a minister she felt would change my life. She constantly invited me to youth night events at her church. One day I accepted the invitation which opened up a new dimension of my life. I was reintroduced to a childhood acquaintance. Was this the man who was supposed to change my life? I had my doubts but I did notice that he had grown into an attractive and well-spoken man of God. As God would have it, that night changed my perception of that young man and the role he would soon fulfill in my life. We became the best of friends. We spoke to each other every day. God was the center of all of our conversations. We worshipped together, he prayed with me and for me daily. My heart grew to love his humor, his protective ways, and his charismatic spirit which drew people to him. Our friendship evolved into a powerful and purposeful relationship. I found great joy in knowing how much he loved me. Yes he loved me so much, so a year later we were married.

Everything happened so fast. We did not plan for it but within a few months I found myself pregnant. I cannot say I was excited about the pregnancy because my plan was that we would travel and get to spend time together before bringing children in the world. The momentum of life began to pick up speed. I was a mother at age 22 and was thrown into being a divorced single parent at 24 years old. What just happened?! We both grew up in the church, how could we fail? How could God fail us and our marriage? Why is my family all broken up? I did the right thing. I got saved, I married a man of God, not to mention he was the love of my life, but somehow our love did not stand the test of time. I asked God why this happened to me but I did not receive an answer; all I heard was silence. My heart was broken and I felt betrayed by love…and yes I know God is love, but somehow God failed me. I did not feel anything in particular, I only felt numb and a massive void. Betrayal, hurt, pain, and shame became the core of my being. Rejection plagued my soul; I was hopeless and my spirit was broken. I now wore the stigma of divorce and fell victim to the phrase, "What did you do to make him leave?" God did not speak to me during this time, however this is when I began to talk to God. I could not figure out where I went wrong: I was living right, going to church, serving and doing my best to be holy. In spite of marrying a preacher, how is it that I ended up living as a divorced single parent?

I had a broken heart, a broken home and a broken spirit. So this was what it felt like to be broken...one never knows until it happens to them. I came from a two parent home, what did I know about being a single parent? My mother was a stay at home mother while my father provided for the six children they created. We were a happy family, and I couldn't ask for a better life. My father and brothers stepped in and assumed the positive male role model for my daughter. My father was my daughter's hero; he would do anything for her. Unfortunately a little over a year after my divorce, we found out my father had terminal cancer. My spirit was shattered. I was 25 when I lost my father; it was a big loss and a big blow to the family. We did not realize how much our father held the family together until he was gone. One life was lost yet it adversely affected the family so much that everyone scattered and lost touch for approximately ten years. We had no idea that my father was the adhesive that held the family together, mentally, physically and financially. We took him for granted in more ways than one can imagine.

The Fight

My father filled in the gap and treated my daughter as his own. He had a special love for his grandchildren, but I was now broken by the loss of the only man who genuinely loved me. There is nothing like the love of a father especially for his daughters. That loss affected me deeply. In sharing this story I must say I am a dreamer, a believer and an achiever. As I grieved the loss of my husband, God was preparing me for the loss of my father. I'm not sure how God works with other people but He shows me things that are meant just for me. Every now and then I'll have dreams that impact other people's lives, such as a birth or a warning of things that will happen in the future...but when the dream was brought to me about my father losing his life, I was in complete denial. Fortunately I was in the habit of telling one person my dreams so when they came true I would have credibility and wouldn't be considered crazy. Six months after I had the dream about losing my father, my mother called me and told me my father had cancer and he had six months to live. I called my brother and told him the news; I asked him if he remembered my dream. His response was yeah, I do but we still have time. I said yeah but that dream was about six months ago, plus when a doctor gives a person time, they don't know! Six days later my father passed away and for my mother all hell broke loose.

People have different ways of mourning and grieving. No one in my family seemed to mourn or grieve the same way. I turned to alcohol; I had to numb my senses because I didn't want to feel the feelings I felt. I only wanted to sleep in hopes of seeing my father again. I had a couple of dreams that were more real than life itself of him coming back to comfort me and to let me know he was in a good place, he wasn't in pain, he was smiling at me. It was like a silent film only in the absence of the words I understood everything he was expressing to me. There were clouds around him and a door, and by the end of the dream he walked through the door. That was the last vision I had, all other contact from that day until now comes in the form of an ordinary dream of which I am still today happy to have. After driving under the influence in a blacked out state, I finally gave up on drinking for a time. My father passed away in June, and at that time I was working for the school district. In some ways the timing was perfect because I had the entire summer to drown myself in my sorrows. The alcohol served as a numbing agent, I didn't want to feel the pain of my loss. After a night of partying and drinking I drove over forty miles in a drunken stupor, with two other passengers in my car. I drove a stick shift and by the grace of God we made it to our destination without incident. All I remember of the entire drive home was singing a line out of a Michael Jackson song, and falling up the stairs to the room where I was sleeping and passing out next to my daughter. The next day I woke up and realized I had a daughter who needed me; I had to get my life back on track. That summer is one big blur, but God was there in spite of the silence.

I am floating over my body, peering down on my physical self. I am lying on the futon in my living room; my body is limp and lifeless. My three year old daughter is nearby, she is sprawled out on the floor watching her favorite Disney movie, *Cinderella.* She has drifted off into fairyland and the television is now watching her, and so am I. I am levitating in the corner of my living room, through no will of my own; there is a spiritual being that has charge over my spirit, and he is controlling my entire being. This is not his first visit, but I panic anyway because this is never a normal occurrence.

I have come to know this force as a gentle spirit from God; his presence embodies strength, peace, compassion and love. I cannot tell you why I know he is a male, but I know with all surety it is so. I am not able to describe the features of this being; all I know is our spirits agree. I do not know the reason, nor do I ever know the reasons for the visitation but I am always enlightened by the end of the time together. Our communication is exchanged in silence; it is a type of telepathy and a unique knowing. I pray I will embrace the message that is being sent. As I stated earlier, this is not the first encounter. I call him The Observer. We never received a formal introduction, but he often visits me and reveals to me many of the blessings God has in store for me. The Observer is like an angel that watches over me, but why is he here now? Why am I peering down at my body? Why is my spirit outside of my body? Anxiety begins to overtake me and suddenly my soul is soothed by a supernatural comfort. The comfort is too great to resist so I embrace it.

In an instant I am whisked off to another realm. No time has passed, no travelling, we are just in another time and place. There is an audience of faceless spirits. I am on a large stage overlooking a giant screen similar to screens at a drive in movie. A baby appears on the screen, and I wonder who is that? The answer comes with a smile. The Observer replies, "That is you." I had never seen myself as a newborn, I never saw any baby pictures of me, and so I marvel at the image. I soon begin to recognize different stages of my life: scenes of my life, the memories are coming fast, flashing in an instant right before my eyes. The images come quickly but the memories bring pain and shame that pierce my spirit. I begin to panic, as the horror floods my soul. Oh my God is this it...is this judgment?! A hollow scream is all I can hear as I cry uncontrollably. I look at the brokenness of my life and I feel sorry I was ever born. Right at the pinnacle of pain it's as if God turned up love in my life. My spirit is now focusing on the love of God. Suddenly I feel ready to die, ready to resign from the world. I truly understand the bible verse, it is better "to be absent from the body and present with the Lord" **2 Corinthians 5:6,** because nothing compares to the love I feel. Suddenly my life has direction and purpose. As I live and love through all of the pain that I must go through and grow through, I know that God is always there for me. My faith in God has allowed me the flexibility and boldness to face all of the obstacles life brings before me. There is so much more to share, but this is the beginning of being whole.

I was still in love with a man who didn't want to have anything to do with me. Be on the lookout for my solo book coming soon.

Marilyn A Waters Biography

Author

Marilyn A Waters was born in San Francisco and was primarily raised in Daly City, California, also known as the Gateway to the Peninsula. Marilyn enjoys traveling locally and abroad, but she has great appreciation for the climate and the culture of the Bay Area. Marilyn was born into a family of six children. Marilyn found balance in life and faith by way of her father's work and her mother's religious beliefs. Marilyn passionately believes in sharing messages of hope, because it is hope that carried her through many struggles in her life. Four years after marrying the love of her life and mothering a daughter, Marilyn found herself divorced and felt abandoned by love. Over time Marilyn discovered that true love is only found in Christ.

Marilyn is a creative at heart, and loves working in the capacity of the creative arts. In 2008 Marilyn wrote and co-produced a radio series called Love Letters to The Lord which aired on KDIA & KDYA in the San Francisco Bay Area. The show was well received and it was a great experience for Marilyn to publicly share stories of hope. 2018 is the year Marilyn picks up the pen and begins again. Stay tuned.

I COMPLETE ME

Listening To GOD Through the Chatter

By

Holly Cranshaw

Published Author~Mortgage Loan Officer~ Fabulous State Licensed Esthetician

Sister~Mother~Aunt~Grandmother~Great Friend to a Few

When you say the words, I Complete Me, it should be a liberating feeling. It should make you feel in control. This chapter addresses one of the things we all deal with, and that is the chatter in our heads. The chatter I like to call GOD trying to get me/us to listen to him.

We all know there is chaos before the blessing, and in this chapter I give insight as to how I am learning to understand and actually listen to the whispers.

When things do not go the way we want them to or we do not get what we perceive is "our gift", the "job" or the "significant other", it's God's way of saying, I've got something greater for you and if you are patient, you will see. The wait will be worth it. Let God bring it together.

I can open doors no man can close and close doors no man can open.

> **Revelation 3:8** [8]I know your deeds. See, I have placed before you an **open** door that **no** one **can** shut. I know that you have little strength, yet you have kept my word and have not denied my name. (Bible– New International Version)

Note from the author: I really want people to use my chapter as a "reference guide", not just a light read. A chapter to review from time to time to get back on track and stay motivated. Teach yourself how to stay present and calm.

It took me 20 years to understand and know what the words "I COMPLETE ME" truly mean. I was never one of those young girls that dreamed of a "prince", the marriage and the white picket fence, so not all little girls dream of that. That was probably because my dad was very strict and his driving force was education and sports (staying out of trouble).

I had this crush on a boy; in I think it was kindergarten, Leconte' Elementary in San Francisco, CA. His name was Chip (laughing) and he lived either across the street or down the street. It was innocent. I could play outside with him (red light, green light) and go to his house when his mom was home, very innocent.

Junior high school, that was painful. Some girl who would do more for him took my boyfriend away. Seriously, I was 13 or 14. "What do you besides hold hands?", that was a question I asked myself.

Moving on, high school, nothing to see, keep moving, same mess, and my boyfriend broke up with me for a girl who again would do more than I would (sex).

So by now, I start to think, what is up with me? Those issues of "abandonment" were real and I would not know why I felt the way I did and had for so long until much later in my life.

Engagement - I called off two weddings because I did not know the meaning of "conflict resolution". At that time in my life, I did not know how to compromise or reconcile. My peaceful ending was to leave at the sign of anything that I did not like. You have to remember, I was raising a son on my own, so it was about him. My son came first.

Leaving situations that make you feel uncomfortable, not a bad thing at all. I am sure some of us would look back and change a few greens lights to red or at least yellow. Never mind, some of us run yellow lights, and many of us who made those U-turns (me) now know that looking over our shoulder and taking a moment to think about the entire situation would have allowed us to continue to go straight ahead.

There are things you have to address when you are truly ready to be happy and content with your life. I am not saying that you must regret anything, but just be honest with at least yourself. No one needs to know your shame/mistakes but GOD and your occasional glass of wine (smiling).

Philippians 3:13-15 [13]Brothers and sisters, I do not consider myself yet to have taken hold of it. But one thing I do: Forgetting what is behind and straining toward what is ahead, [14]I press on toward the goal to win the prize for which God has called me heavenward in Christ Jesus. [15]All of us, then, who are mature, should take such a view of things. And if on some point you think differently, that too God will make clear to you. (Bible - New International Version)

I am worth more than I thought

The time I thought I was missing out is when most of my friends were going out and meeting young boys/men. I was never a big partier. I was not allowed to "hang-out" and party. I was allowed to go to school homecomings and events, roller skating and a club with my brother that was called California Hall. Now that was fun; dancing and having fun with my brother and extended family.

I realized I really did not like going out because young men would not ask me to dance. The young men that did were not that cute, but I danced and had fun. That taught me it was about having fun. I decided I liked staying home and there is nothing wrong with that or me. I was looking for something I already had but I did not know what that was.

> **Acts 20-24** However, I consider my life worth nothing to me; my only aim is to finish the race and complete the task Lord Jesus have given me – the task of testifying to the good news of God's grace. (Bible - New International Version)

If you are honest with yourself, we as females compare our lives, careers and relationships to our friends and family. The issue or problem with that is, we only see the outside, and we do not see what goes on behind closed doors. If you listen to what "society" shows us and tells us, depending on where you are in life - single, divorced, owning a home before you are 30 or living with your partner out of "wed-lock" - you may feel like you are "not complete".

I feel people who live with that mindset of emptiness or wanting more to feel complete in certain situations do not know that only they can make themselves complete. When you are truly complete, you have peace of mind and you love having alone time.

Philippians 4:13 I CAN DO all things through him who gives me strength. (Bible - New International Version)

Discovering the sweetness of the "chatter"

I remember when I could not ride in my car without music. I would try, really I would, but the chatter in my head would start to take place. It would sound so confusing and loud at times; it sounded like when you press fast forward on a cassette player to find that verse you like, you know what I mean. I just figured my mind was racing with thoughts and things I needed to do. I needed something in the background to drown out all the chatter, so I eventually turned on the radio. At that time, I would have never thought that the "chatter in my head" was God talking to me, trying to get my attention. Wanting to help me, to give me some answers to questions I asked and possibly prayed about. When you are going through things, you think the voices you hear make you crazy. That is something we are taught. You are crazy if you have voices in your head. Don't get me wrong, some of those voices NEED TO BE SILENCED. I am talking about God, not the Devil and his poisonous rants. I found out that the chatter was calmness, answers to questions, visions of what is next or what could be. When I stopped to listen to the chatter, it sounded like a violin concert on a warm beach, listening to water hitting the rocks. That is what my God wanted and needed me to hear, and as the violin concert faded out, I could hear and start to understand some of the words that God was so desperately trying to get me to listen to.

> **Proverbs 2:1-5** [1]My son, if you accept my words and store up my commands within you, [2]turning your ear to wisdom and applying your heart to understanding- [3]indeed, if you call out for insight and cry aloud for understanding, [4]and if you look for it as for silver and search for it as for hidden treasure, [5]then you will understand the fear of the LORD **and** find the knowledge of God. (Bible - New International Version)

Now, I first had to learn how to decipher intuition (Gods words), and from there, fear/anxiety/doubt. Fear/anxiety/doubt can be positive if you do not hear it correctly; you can twist it. Fear can be like standing in cement, and life will pass you right on by. What I mean by fear/anxiety/doubt can be positive, you can be in a situation or wanting something specific and not get it. You get annoyed and ask yourself all kinds of questions, making up What If scenarios, not even thinking about the positive side of "not getting" what you want.

God was actually protecting you from something that could have turned out really badly, leaving you in an unnecessary situation.

> **Mark 4:24** And he said to them, "Pay attention to what you hear: with the measure you use, it will be measured to you, and still more will be added to you." (Bible - New International Version)

I took it one step further and started fasting every Thursday. That was the day of the week I decided to just focus on deepening my spiritual mind. It was then I started writing more. At one point in deepening my spiritual mind, I wrote four pages of a book and poems and felt a surge of powerful, positive energy. I felt calm. That is also when I realized certain foods will and can flood your mind in a negative way. I found strength in controlling something in my life: the way I thought and what my thoughts could produce. However, with deepening your spiritual growth comes chaos, which we like to call negative thoughts, negative people, or what some folks call the devil. I often hear some say, when they are on the path to what God has for them, the closer you get, the faster the devil sends his minions out to trip you up, or to detour you and your thoughts. Remember, if the enemy cannot get you coming, he will get you or try to get you finishing. Be ready for the battle. Stay in alignment because the enemy knows your nature.

Philippians 1:6 Being confident of this, that he who began a good work in you will carry it on to completion until the day of Christ Jesus. (Bible - New International Version)

Ephesians 6:11-17 [11]Put on the full armor of God, so that you can take your stand against **the devil**'s schemes. [12]For our struggle is not against flesh and blood, but against the rulers, against the authorities, against the powers of this dark world and against the spiritual forces of evil in the heavenly realms. [13]Therefore put on the full armor of God, so that when the day of evil comes, you may be able to stand your ground, and after you have done everything, to stand. [14]Stand firm then, with the belt of truth buckled around your waist, with the breastplate of righteousness in place, [15]and with your feet fitted with the readiness that comes from the gospel of peace. [16]In addition to all this, take up the shield of faith, with which you can extinguish all the flaming arrows of the evil one. [17]Take the helmet of salvation and the sword of the Spirit, which is the word of God. (Bible - New International Version)

This is what I had to learn how to do, and it was hard and still is challenging at times. Your mind is powerful regardless of positive, negative or resting thoughts. It is a powerful tool if you understand how to use it. You will slip up from time to time, but understand and be very sensitive and PRESENT with your thoughts at all times.

Take for instance this chapter. I have been avoiding it. I felt I could not do it. I was tired; I got sick and was still fighting pneumonia, still on medicine. I had no energy, desire, or motivation to write. She (my mind chatter) was cheering too, she thought she had won. I saw her reclining in a chair, reporting back to her devil. Hey everyone, I have her mind under control, and we are good. This chapter will not be published. This blessing is a wrap.

If I did not write this chapter, I felt I could and would justify it as, "I already accomplished what I wanted, and that was to have a chapter published in a book," *Meeting in the Middle* which was released in January 2018.

God said you are not done; this is the beginning of something. You do not need to know the outcome, JUST WRITE.

It is Monday, March 12, 2018 at 4:06 pm and I started writing this today when I got to work around 10:30am. This is what taking back control of your mind will do for you. God said, do not write a story, write to inspire, to uplift. Base it on how I finally got you to listen to my voice, to understand your journey is not complete, but you are.

Completeness-Closing in

As you got older, you start to realize, I am not missing anything, and I am not lonely or alone. Do not let someone else define those definitions for you. Knowing you feel good depends on you, and let's face it, you can only let yourself down, no one can let you down when you depend on GOD and yourself. Taking care of me and becoming a better version of me is what I strive for every day, and some days I do say, NOT TODAY. Nevertheless, I owe GOD PRAISE, EVERY DAY. It is so easy to say, God woke me up this morning, Amen. Go one-step further and ask Him, why? What is on the agenda today, what do I conquer? When I feel like I need the Lord in my spirit, which is every day, I press CD number 6 and let it run through to the end of number 1 (Marvin Sapp's CD "Thirsty" and "Close"). Number 2 and number 3, that is just Mary and Tamar. lol (wink).

Quick flash back: I can remember every day my grandmother would have 6am prayer and worship call with the members of Bell Chapel Christian Methodist Episcopal Church in San Francisco on Palou Avenue. I never knew why she did that day after day after day at 6am on the dot (The Prayer Line). I now know that it is necessary to pray throughout the day, and it is so easy now to understand why Grandma Nona had 6am prayer and worship.

I will continue to ask for guidance, and to listen for God through the chatter, for Him to show me the path He has for me. Just a glimpse, because let's be honest, that path behind me goes in circles, around the corner, backwards, and now it's time to WALK IN MY BLESSINGS and accept that I Complete Me.

God has been waiting for me to get it together. God waits for all of us to get it together. That little voice that is whispering to you is God. You may think it is just chatter but trust me from firsthand experience, it is not. My entire mind and emotions shift and my spirit comes alive when I turn on my car and hear, I Am Safe In His Arms by Marvin Sapp from his CD "Close." I drive a little different each day.

Then there are those days and times where I feel like, where is GOD? I did not hear Him today, I did not feel Him yet, things are not getting better, and nothing is changing. A moment of uncontrolled anxiety (the devil is cheering, we got her back) I am in a state of wading, resistant to move. I'm upset and yell, God what's up? What's next? and I hear,

It is my timing, not when you want it. Learn to have patience.

Side note – devastating, bad, emotional and drained is how I hear people describe certain events in their lives, and I think to myself, it is not as bad as YOU think. However, that is how they are feeling at that moment about their situation. It is not for me to say you should not feel that way; I am not in their shoes and cannot feel their pain, especially if it is something I have not gone through myself. God's moves are strategic and purposeful.

> **Isaiah 49:14-16** [14]But Zion said, "The LORD has forsaken me, the LORD has forgotten me." [15]"Can a mother forget the baby at her breast and have no compassion on the child she has borne? Though she may forget, I will not forget you! [16]See, I have engraved you on the palms of my **hands**; your walls are ever before me. (Bible - New International Version)

> **Isaiah 41:13** [13]For I am the LORD your God who takes hold of your right hand and says to you, Do not fear; I will help you. (Bible - New International Version)

Can we count how many times God has carried us or do we just remember the times he has gotten us out of a situation? His loving grace is amazing and kind. He really does want to help us, as I said earlier in this chapter; He is WAITING FOR ME/US to come to Him, humbly.

I am thankful for all the circles I made, because it brought me to this place in my spirit. I finally listened and heard God say, your way is not working for you, how about you let me try it my way? (Laughing.)

Always remember, if it is the will of God, it is for you!

I am now learning how to be FACE TO FACE WITH GOD WITH NO limits (Marvin Sapp-Face to Face on his CD "Close").

> **Genesis 32:30** [30]So Jacob called the place Peniel, saying, "It is because I saw God **face to face**, and yet my life was spared." (Bible - New International Version)

> **Exodus 33:11** [11]The LORD would speak to Moses face to face, as one speaks to a friend. Then Moses would return to the camp, but his young aide Joshua son of Nun did not leave the tent. (Bible - New International Version)

I am learning, listening, and growing and so excited about my life and future. I embrace being woken up between 2am and 3am every single morning to hear the answer to a question I had earlier that day or to just feel His presence. It is amazing. The thing is to know it is the answer and not to second-guess God's whispers to you and me. When the whispers get LOUD, you will wish you had taken a little time to do what God told you to do the first time. God's whispers get loud, and you don't want to wait until He has to show you He means business.

I am coming into a phase in my life that is exciting and there is still that thought of oh no, what if I actually succeed? I am by no means perfect and do not have it all together. I do not measure what I have achieved, and not what anyone else has. Certain people do motivate me and I find that such a rush. I find I can push myself and accomplish a goal, cross that off and keep moving forward. I have also learned that my timing and journey is mine, delays and all. Do not be ashamed, do not compare your life to any one person. Compare yourself to no one. (Do not go back into the cement.)

Last night the chatter said, **YOU ARE COMPLETE!**

Bible Study (Bible - New International Version)

<u>Alive in Christ</u>

> **Colossians 2:9-10** For in Christ all the fullness of the Deity dwells in bodily form. 10.<u>And you have been made complete in Christ, who is the head over every ruler and authority.</u> 11.In Him you were also circumcised in the putting off of your sinful nature, with the circumcision performed by Christ and not by human hands....

Finished. 3:47pm on 3/13/2018. We can do all things when we just believe and walk in faith not by sight. (Bible - New International Version)

Holly Cranshaw Biography:

Published Author~Mortgage Loan Officer~ Fabulous State Licensed Esthetician

Sister~Mother~Aunt~Grandmother~Great Friend to a Few

Holly Cranshaw is continuing her writing journey with a new chapter titled, I Complete Me. She is working towards writing and publishing a complete book. Some of the book will be based on the writings and teachings of God: How to stay positive, releasing anxiety and knowing what to do when negative thoughts creep in.

Ephesians 4:22-24 **ESV / English Standard Version**

To put off your old self, which belongs to your former manner of life and is corrupt through deceitful desires, and to be renewed in the spirit of your minds, and to put on the new self, created after the likeness of God in true righteousness and holiness. (ESV- English Standard Version)

Holly has learned that blessings come in all forms. She is learning how to listen to God. She will continue to work on having patience and wait for God's guidance and words. She will know when it is time to move forward and take the next step towards another blessing in her life's journey.

Holly heard God say to her: Remember, if you step back, you will step on my feet; I have on sandals so it will hurt me, not you.

If she has one lesson she feels she's supposed to teach or preach, the lesson would be, understand you cannot expect someone else to make or bring you happiness; THEY cannot make you Complete. Stop hiding.

God is waiting on you.

Accountability is Where Healing Begins

Don't Let the Wrong Person Write Your Life Story

By

Candess S. Barker

Artist~ Author~ Founder of the Colours of Life Art Exhibition.

Facebook @ColoursOL

Email: Coloursolae@gmail.com

"If it weren't for *blank*, I would have *blanked* by now." You could insert almost any noun and verb into these spaces and this would be the reason that my mom's life hadn't turned out the way she wanted it to. For as long as I can remember, I recall her frustrated rants about missed opportunities and the people she held responsible for them.

My mom is a creative, talented woman with great ideas. Yet, for all her great qualities, she has never seemed to find her feet landing exactly where she wanted them to. As a girl I would watch her get all fired up about a new project. The house would be buzzing with the energy from the new venture under way. My sisters and I would be so excited to participate in her new mission. Eager to ride the wave of momentum. Then, about two weeks into the new project the first roadblock would present itself. Her momentum would slow, but as her excited assistants we would be ready to move on to the next step. Our excitement would be enough to push her to find a way around that roadblock. However, when the second and third presented themselves, it would prove to be too much for her and the project would come to an end.

As kids we didn't understand what was standing in our mom's way. To us, if one thing didn't work you just did something else. We hadn't made it to that point in life where people believe quitting is better than trying. We had so much faith in her ability to make things happen, that when she gave up, we wanted to know why. Maybe it was out of frustration, or not wanting to seem like a failure to her kids. Maybe those were the excuses she gave herself for not being able to achieve her full potential. Whatever the reason, she usually told us it was because some person or circumstance stood in her way.

My mom is nothing if not a woman of great ingenuity. She raised eight children in a low-income household in Oakland. So, there was no end to her resourcefulness when our basic needs were in question. I am more than grateful to have inherited her many skills to stretch, conserve and improvise.

It seems, though, as long as the road block stood between my mom and her dreams, she just couldn't muster up the courage to push through the adversity. Sadly, just as many other children of parents with broken and left behind dreams, I too inherited this behavior of self-doubt, fear of success, self-sabotage and blame.

I don't think my mom believed the excuses she gave us. I think deep down she knew they were just that, excuses. But over time, she actually began to believe that she had no control over the direction her life took. At this point the excuse she told herself was, "It just wasn't meant to be." And eventually it became, "It wasn't God's will."

Where this whole idea of "It wasn't meant to be" originated, I'm not sure. Maybe it came from the idea of fate or that we all have a predestined path and end to our lives. Maybe it developed out of a human need to distance ourselves from our shortcomings. What I now know it to be is a long-told excuse for a lack of success and a subconscious mantra of failure that, if unchecked, can have a lasting effect spanning generations. I was only about 5 or 6 years old when this notion of a higher power intervening in or blocking your forward progress started to creep into my subconscious mind. I had heard my mother's frustrated sighs of "It wasn't meant to be" enough times to start believing that we as humans had no control over what the universe or God dished out to us. I was burdened with this belief that either you were fortunate and the universe granted you this great life or you weren't. Adversely, I was taught that God's people were meek and lived humble lives free of material entrapments and consequently, the poor were more favored by God. Even then this didn't sit well with me because I couldn't understand why God would want his people to suffer.

My mom isn't a believer of fate or luck. In fact, as a child I was banned from engaging in anything that had to do with luck or fate. I was told that the idea of destiny was absurd because only God could say how your life would play out. This was confusing because after all, didn't "It wasn't meant to be" mean that there was a predestined plan for your life that couldn't be altered? And what about God? Didn't God want us to be happy? So why wouldn't he grant us favor over the things that would improve our lives? Despite all the logic in me even at such a young age. My mom's words still carried such weight because as a child your mom's words might as well be God's. No one has to tell you to believe in every word your mom says. You just do.

I'm not sure how far back in our family's history this belief system goes. I don't know much about my mother's childhood. I've never met my grandparents. My mom's relationship with her mother was strained from before I was born up until her mother passed a few years ago for very much the same reason that my relationship with her is almost non-existent today. What I do know from the information that I've been given about my grandmother is that she was an outgoing woman. However, there was something missing, a barrier to entry that could not be passed. The same is evident in my mom's life and so on with me and my siblings. My grandmother or "my mother's mom" as we so distantly called her ended her days with her family in turmoil, saddled with guilt, confessing her shortcomings to her children. I intend to break this cycle for me and my daughter and those who will come after her.

The first step to breaking the cycle is recognizing the pattern.

It was at the end of my first year of college that I realized I was a **half-asser**. I remember having a conversation with my older sister about the fact that I wished I could give 100% effort in my studies. If I had the ability, I would be an amazing artist. I had recognized my pattern of getting an assignment: Thinking of all the things I could include that would impress my professor, how great my presentation would be, and then the doubt would set in. "There's a lot of research involved. What if I don't know what to write? What if I can't produce a drawing? What if my work isn't as good as everyone else's?" Then to rid myself of these painful thoughts, I would tell myself I had time. I would put the assignment off until the last minute and then a day or two before it was due I would go into **"Oh, Sh*t"** mode.

I would sit down and with the impending deadline looming over me, I would push those thoughts out of my mind and write or draw at a feverish pace, producing a work of art or essay that would impress even myself. *To say that I am struggling with this hard-fought habit even now as I write is an understatement!* But as my courses got harder and life continued to happen, this method of procrastinating and sprinting to the finish would not carry me through the remainder of my studies. Eventually, they became too much for me. Together with a demanding job, a three-year-old and an active divorce...I succumbed to the "It wasn't meant to be" syndrome and so continued the cycle.

As I stated before, I was 5 or 6 when this way of thinking began to affect me. I remember being in kindergarten. I was in my room lying back on my bed. I could hear the bustle of my family throughout the rest of the house. I thought to myself how fortunate I was that I had both of my parents, all my siblings, and a big beautiful home. How incredibly favored I felt. This memory that hangs so vividly in my mind even now was the last time in my life that I felt completely secure.

Shortly after this all the things that I felt incredibly favored to have begun to fall away. My parents got divorced and my dad moved out. My brother became a juvenile delinquent and began terrorizing our family. We had to leave the comfort of the home that most of us were born in and sleep from house to house, living with my mom's friends. We would go to school in the morning with all our belongings piled in the back of our station wagon. I felt such guilt over that one happy thought I'd had. Over bragging to myself how fortunate we were. It seems illogical now, but as a 6-year-old child I held myself responsible for the welfare of my family. With the belief system that I had inadvertently been taught, I reasoned that I was unlucky and therefore susceptible to more misfortune in the future. Also, I believed that everything had been perfectly fine in my life until I thought of how perfect it was. Maybe God was punishing me for my smugness and maybe I had to suffer to win back his favor. Needless to say, this created a whole host of other issues for me mentally and emotionally in my adult life.

Up until my late 20's, through many ups and downs, I held fast to this belief that God put me on this earth to suffer. For example, there are times in particular such as my rocky marriage and a three-year bout with infertility before my daughter was born. I felt incredibly hated by God, even to the point that I stopped praying. During this time, even though we weren't on speaking terms I still felt his presence. This led me into one of my darkest times where I asked, "Why doesn't he just let me die?" Thankfully though, I made it through that dark time. And on the other side, some years later. I understood why he never left. I needed time on my own to learn what his love was, because I had already been brainwashed with what it wasn't. With the conception of my daughter I rekindled my relationship with God and vowed never to give him the silent treatment again. After the birth of my daughter, my view of God's purpose for me changed. She was a symbol that I wasn't put here to suffer and that there was a greater purpose for me, something I had always known but never felt worthy of the task. So much so that about a year ago when a co-worker *(Ms. Sheila Price)* asked me if I had ever asked God for his favor, I had to admit that the thought never occurred to me. I'd never felt worthy enough to ask for something that felt so selfish. She reassured me that if I asked, he would listen. So, I did and I have never felt so free. I am forever grateful for the conversation we had that day.

Around the time of my daughter's birth I began to question my mother's belief system and all the excuses became clear to me. I vowed to begin changing all the things that had made me feel so worthless growing up for my daughter's sake. Yet I still did not fully understand what made me feel this way. It would be many years yet to come until I uncovered what the missing piece of the puzzle was to set my life on the right course. For now, I had made a breakthrough. Yet, I remained reserved through the good times. Still waiting for the other shoe to drop.

It's your puzzle. You're responsible for putting it back together.

"You can't win for losing." This is one of my mom's sayings that has always perplexed me. It's like asking which came first, the chicken or the egg. The funny thing is that I've said it before even though I had no clue what it meant. I just knew it was something my mom said when something went wrong despite her best efforts. When I caught myself using this idiom, it caused me to pause. First because I really had no idea why I was using it. Second because it just didn't add up. If you couldn't win...for losing? Then it stands to say that you were going to lose from the beginning. If that's the case. Why would you even try?

There it was. The missing piece of the puzzle. A self-fulfilling prophecy. I now know why my mom is a *quitter* and why I'm a *half-asser*. As humans we naturally have the drive to do something bigger than ourselves, but that will only carry you so far. If your belief system is built upon a predisposed idea that you are insignificant in this world, then every step you take will lead you toward fulfilling that thought which you have already set into motion. No amount of blame will change the course that you set. It will only delay the disappointment, stirring up feelings of insecurity and self-loathing that are bound to affect those around you.

The thing about blame is, it's all imaginary anyway. When you place blame on someone, it doesn't affect them unless they acknowledge or take responsibility for it. It does affect you however. When you assign blame, whether it be a person, circumstance or higher power, you also make them responsible for correcting the path that you laid out. In doing so, you also give up control over the outcome. You allow the wrong person to write your life story.

On the surface, the blame we lay on others alleviates us from the immediate discomfort of failure. But on a deeper level we are unconsciously brainwashing ourselves to self-sabotage, give up and fail. I don't think my mom knew the harm she was doing when she blamed others and made excuses. In fact, I believe most parents think they are helping to soothe their children when they tell them these falsehoods. I believe my mom did the best she could with the tools she was given. She may have had her own ideas about how she would change our lives from that of what she experienced growing up. But when we as parents are not honest with ourselves, we not only sabotage our children; we strip them of the secure foundation and grounding within themselves that they will need in the future to allow them to enter the world and become thriving adults, unafraid and unapologetic for who they are and who they want to become.

A person may not care that you blame them. A circumstance is just that, a circumstance. It can't respond to or take responsibility for itself. It's up to you to make the best of it. The universe will only reflect back the energy that you send out. As for God, He is here to guide us. He watches over us as we walk along the path we choose. Pointing out pitfalls and shining light down when we ask for it. He lets us make our own missteps to allow us to learn. And when we ask for stamina to carry us through our journey, He provides it. He wills us to do that which we have already set our minds upon.

If you want to change your path, change your prophecy. Your destiny begins and ends inside your own mind. You are the author of your own life story.

"When we are stuck in whose fault something is, we are trapped in victim mode. The road to power is in taking responsibility. Your heart, your life, your happiness is your responsibility and your responsibility alone."

~Will Smith~

Candess S. Barker Biography

Artist~ Author~ Founder of the Colours of Life Art Exhibition.

Candess S. Barker was born and raised in Oakland, CA as the middle child of eight siblings. She studied Animation & Visual Effects at Ex'pression College for New Media. She is a proud graduate of the Women's Initiative Business Program, where she developed her business plan for Passion for Elegance Event Planning.

Candess has always been passionate about creating art that addresses emotional, personal, and social issues as well as bringing consciousness and empowerment to women and people of color. In her endeavor for personal growth and community building, she founded the Colours of Life Art Exhibition in 2015.

As a firm believer in women empowering other women to love, believe in, and find themselves, Candess takes every opportunity to encourage women and young girls, starting at home with her spirited 13-year-old daughter Jayde.

Her continuous mission for self-awareness and fulfillment of her life's purpose with the support of her loving fiance' Jai has led Candess to begin mentoring young women and participating in speaking engagements to inspire other women to find their own purpose.

Treasure Hidden In Darkness

By

Christina Aguilar

Age 34

Author~ Speaker~ Mother~ Wife

www.christinaaguilar33.wixsite.com/author

Email: achristina628@gmail.com

"I can do all things through Christ who strengthens me."

Philippians 4:13 (NIV)

Hi, my name is Christina Aguilar I'm a mother, wife, speaker, co-author of Breaking Through Barriers Vol2/Broken Into Brilliance Vol1. In these books I share my testimonies of how my life was before Christ when I was in the world.

First, of all I would like to give thanks to my Father in Heaven for giving me this opportunity to show His people how much He loves us. No one, not even the devil, can break our chains like God can. Our God is mighty and strong. He loves everyone unconditionally. I pray that my story encourages you to trust God with all your heart; give him all the areas that you feel ashamed to talk about.

When I was in darkness, I had no identity. Instead, I carried many labels such as bisexual, lesbian, drug addict, alcoholic, angry, insecure, selfish and willing to try anything, etc. When I looked in the mirror, I was empty on the inside. I had no convictions; to be honest, I was very miserable. I look back now and think, how could I put myself in those situations? I wanted love but really didn't even know what love was or even loved myself. The devil had me blinded. When you're spiritually blind you can't see Christ because you hardened your heart and won't come to the knowledge of the Truth. Everyone knows God's real, but people reject Him because they love their sin and don't want to submit to him. Then Satan comes into the picture and blinds the minds of the Unbelievers so they won't come to the truth. When you're spiritually blind you are separated from God and you will continue to lie to yourself: God's not real, the Bible is false, hell is fake, I'm a good person, Jesus was just a man, etc. 2 Corinthians4:4 (NLT) Satan, who is the god of this world, has blinded the minds of those who don't believe. They are unable to see the glorious light of the Good News. They don't understand this message about the glory of Christ, who is the exact likeness of God.

Isaiah 45:3-7 (NKJV)

I will give the treasures of darkness and hidden riches of secret places, that you may know that I, the lord, Who call you by name, am the God of Israel. For Jacob my servant's sake and Israel my elect, I have even called you by your name; I have named you, though you have not known me. I am the Lord God, and there is no other; there is no God besides me. I will gird you, though you have not known me, that they may know from the rising of the sun to its setting that there is none besides me. I am the Lord, and there is no other; I form the light and create darkness, I make peace and create calamity; I the Lord, do all these things."

WHO I AM WITH CHRIST

Well now when I look in the mirror I see a beautiful, brave, courageous, mighty woman of God. Jesus helped me with everything. He gave me purpose, he took all my hurts and pains away, and He took away all the labels that the world gave me. I got delivered from many demons that had me in bondage for a long time. I had to surrender everything to God. I remember having many mental battles; my flesh was used to doing its own thing. I realized that I needed to read my Bible and pray have a real relationship with God.

There are times when Satan likes to remind me of the person I use to be. He shoots fiery darts like fears, doubts and not being good enough. Even in my dreams. But I have to rebuke him in Jesus' name. He is a liar. Everything he ever told me wasn't true. Now I focus on God and his promises for my life. I know He loves me and I'm very grateful for everything He has done in my life.

James 1:22-25(NKJV)

But be doers of the Word, and not hearers only deceiving yourselves. For if anyone is a hearer of the Word and not a doer, he is like a man observing his natural face in a mirror; For he observes himself, goes away, and immediately forgets what kind of man he was. But he who looks into perfect law of liberty and continues in it, and is not a forgetful hearer but a doer of the work, this one will be blessed in what he does.

WHO IS OUR GOD?

Our Father wishes that we would draw near to know him better, to experience His presence and learn His voice, just as it is one thing to know about fire and quite another to experience its light, warmth, and burn. God invites us to know Him, not just about Him. Here are a few things we know of God with supreme certainty because this is how He introduces Himself throughout the scripture:

Without Rival by Lisa Bevere

I AM...one. Deut.6:4, Mark 12:29, Gal. 3:20, 1Tim.2:5, James 2:19

IAM...the Alpha and the Omega. Rev.1:8, 21:6;22:13

IAM...WHO I AM. Exod. 3:14

IAM...from everlasting to everlasting. 1Chron. 16:36

IAM...the author and finisher of your faith. Heb.12:2

IAM...the creator of heaven and Earth. Gen 1:1

IAM...able. Matt. 3:9

IAM...Love. 1John 4:7_8,16

IAM...good. Mark 10:18, Luke 18:19, 1Tim .4:4

IAM...among you in your midst. Deut 6:15, Luke17:21, 1Cor.14:25

IAM...truth and true. John 3:33

IAM...Your Healer. Exod. 15:26

IAM...Spirit. John 4:24

IAM...Father. John 6:46, Phil. 2:11

IAM...glorified in the son. John 13:31

IAM...your witness. Rom. 1:9, Phil. 1:8, 1Thess. 2:5

IAM...revealed. Rom. 1:17

IAM...for you. Rom. 8:31

IAM...Over all. Rom. 9:5, Eph. 4:6

IAM...merciful. Deut. 4:31, Rom. 12:1

IAM...faithful. 1Cor. 1:9, 10:13, 2Cor. 1:18

IAM...wiser than men. 1Cor. 1:25

IAM...not the author of confusion. 1Cor. 14:33

IAM...the author of peace. 1Cor. 14:33

IAM...your sufficiency. 2Cor. 3:5

IAM...gracious and generous. Exod.34, Neh. 9

IAM...slow to anger. Joel 2:13, Nah. 1:3

IAM...highly exalted. Phil 2:9

IAM...working in you. Phil 2:13

IAM...invisible. Col. 1:15

IAM...the God who is coming. Col. 3:6

IAM…the righteous judge. 2 Thess. 1:5

IAM…Savior of all people.1Tim. 2:3, 4:10

IAM…unbound. 2 Tim. 2:9

IAM…The builder of all things. Heb.3:4

IAM…just. Heb. 6:10

IAM…Alive. Heb. 10:31

IAM…a consuming fire. Deut.6:3, Heb.12:29

IAM…light.1John 1:5

IAM…greater than your hearts.1John 3:20

IAM…the God who is, and was, and is to come. Rev 1:18

IAM…holy. Rev11:17

IAM…your strength. Exod.15:2

IAM…your song. Exod. 15:2

IAM…jealous. Exod. 34:14, Deut. 4:24

IAM…not a man. Num.23:19, Deut. 4:24

IAM…God of gods and lord of lords. Deut. 10:17

IAM…great, mighty, and awesome. Deut.10:17

IAM…not partial. Deut. 10:17

IAM…your praise. Deut. 10:21

IAM…with you in battle. Deut. 20:4

IAM…a warrior. Exod.15:3

IAM…your dwelling place. Deut. 33:27

IAM…your rock and refuge. 2 Sam .22:32-33

IAM…God alone. Deut.4:32, 35 Kings 8:60

Well I'm currently involved in the hope center recovery program at my church, Praise chapel in Antioch CA. It gives me joy to help people to show them what God can do in their lives. And in the future I would love to continue to write books, speak at events, be a better mom, wife, sister, friend and just continue to serve God with all my heart. I know God has great plans for my life that are bigger than me. I love God with all my heart; He is my everything and He showed me that I'm someone special, that I'm beautiful inside and out. I'm in the process of working on my solo book… So stay tuned…

It is not fancy hair, gold jewelry, or fine clothes that should make you beautiful.

No, your beauty should come from inside you- the beauty of a gentle and quiet spirit. That beauty will never disappear, and it is worth very much to God.

1 Peter 3:3-4

Christina Aguilar Biography

Author~ Speaker~ Mother~ Wife

Christina Aguilar is a 34 years old mother and wife. She was born and raised in Pittsburg California. Christina grew up in a single–parent home. Her father was absent from her life as he battled a drug addiction. During her childhood, Christina struggled with feeling alone, especially without having her father present. Feeling alone and unloved while trying to fill her fatherless void led Christina down a path of drug addiction and self-destruction. After years of ups and downs, Christina was invited to a church that would change her life. She gave church a chance and found out that the love she was looking for was in Jesus. She gives all thanks to Jesus for mending her broken heart and allowing her to finally move past her past by releasing the pain she held inside. She received deliverance from all addictions and strong holds that held her back in life. In January 2017, Christina became a 1st time author; she is featured in Breaking Through Barriers Volume2 and in Broken Into Brilliance. Christina aspires to show others that they can overcome their past and have a brighter future. Through her testimony, books, and future speaking engagements, Christina hopes to motivate others to trust and love God. Christina feels very thankful and gives God all the glory for the wonderful changes in her life.

"I Didn't Want to Die"

By

Teresa Dye

Author~ Wife~ Mother~ Grandmother~ Survivor

Age 56

Pittsburg, CA

Contact me: whytedyemunds@aol.com

Find Me:

TeresaLynn@GodLovesMeSo

Stay tuned for my solo book, currently in the planning stages!

I would need more hands and toes than I have to count the number of times in my life I have heard the remark, "You should write a book". These remarks are not made because I possess any proven talent for writing. These remarks or recommendations are made because of the hurdles in my life I have had to jump over. Most would characterize these events in my life as a collective tragedy or a horror story, but I call them hurdles because I just have to jump high enough to get over the hurdle.

Let me give you a brief history of my life up until now so that you, the reader, can put into context the story I am about to tell.

I was born to a very dysfunctional couple. I came prematurely after my father (allegedly) threw my mother down a set of stairs. My parents were both psychologically damaged in ways that I will never fully comprehend. When I was conceived they were divorced, and they remarried before my birth only to divorce again shortly after I was born. My mother went on to remarry again; the first of my many step fathers would become the nightmare that would shape so much of the life I was yet live. He was a rapist. He was my initial abuser. The sexual abuse I experienced at his hands would go on for almost a decade. When a child is violated in such a way, before that child is even old enough to attend kindergarten, well, it leaves damage. It left me with what I call an invisible

"V" on my forehead. "V" for victim. Normal people could not see the "V"; they could see the me that I let the world see. My "V" was visible to predators. Predators saw the "V" and immediately knew the vulnerability that came with it. My life would include multiple violations by multiple predators, violations of my flesh and psyche that would not end until I decided to end me.

As dramatic as that may sound, that is the truth. I was a single mother of 2. By the grace of God I had landed a great job with a great company, let's call that company Gifco*. Gifco hired me when I was 19 years old. I honestly never thought I could get a job. I had not graduated high school. My life being the crazy mess it was, I could not even recall the last grade I had completed. My friend encouraged me to apply for the position and on a lark I did. I boldly lied on my application by indicating I had graduated from high school. I eventually got the job. My first positon was mail and file clerk. Over the next 13 ½ years I had many supervisors and managers. I was promoted many times to better paying positions within Gifco, and then I reached a plateau. At the time the managing staff of my department did not see me as having the image Gifco wished to project, so promoting me further into a position that would put me in direct contact with the business world outside our building, and thus reflect poorly on the company, was not going to happen. I did not fit the mold the powers that be thought I should. That would change. With all companies people move on and staff changes. I got a new supervisor. Let's call him Cal*. Cal saw my potential and counseled me to pursue advancement. Under his tutelage I was promoted to a highly respected and coveted positon within the company. Life was pretty good. I was still a single mother but I was finally able to provide for my daughters in a manner that I was proud of.

Things would soon change yet again. After years with Cal as my boss I had flourished. Cal had become my friend and I had mixed socially with his wife and kids. Then a rumor began to spread within Gifco that the company was up for sale. Upon a sale, none of us could be guaranteed our jobs. There was a quiet panic among the staff. The powers that be denied the rumors and all seemed to calm down. Shortly thereafter, Cal gave his notice of termination. He told some of us that he was going to Livorna*. Cal stated he had received an inside tip from a friend employed at the Gifco home office that Gifco was indeed up for sale. Cal had a family to support and could not risk being unemployed. Still, I refused to believe the rumors. Cal settled into his leadership role at Livorna. Cal called me several times to offer me a position with Livorna. Apparently he had touted me as the answer to a need there within his department. He had also promised Livorna that he could persuade me to take the job. As a favor to Cal I interviewed with his boss Joe*. Joe was a very unassuming man and repeatedly increased his offer to entice me to accept the job. I declined. I had no desire to quit one job and take another based on the same lie. Cal was steadfast in his efforts; he repeatedly and vigorously encouraged me to accept the offer. He pushed on for an explanation as to why I continued to decline his offer. I admitted to him that I had lied on my application. He encouraged me, telling me he believed I was better able to do "the job" than other college educated persons. He also made clear that he would be my boss and no one had to know I did not graduate from high school, as he would be taking care of my application. Still I declined. Months later at an industry seminar, the speaker used Gifco as an example of big employers leaving California due to the cost of doing business there. The truth was out. My company was up for sale. Suffice it to say, I called Cal and accepted the job offer from Livorna.

Day one at my new job: Cal picked me up at my home as I would take possession of my company car that day. It was an amazing day. As luck would have it, it was employee appreciation day. I spent that day with my new coworkers enjoying a BBQ and festivities. Luck was not on my side when it came to the company car. My car was still being used by another employee, so Cal had to give me a ride home. He came in to talk about my new job. After much dialogue, he moved closer to give me a hug. It was awkward. Then, in a matter of seconds he was upon me. The abuse had begun; it was groping and the like for the time being. I immediately fell easily into the victim role. I was familiar with that territory. When I pulled away from Cal and told him I was not comfortable with this activity he told be that as long as I made him happy, my job was safe. Cal was able to facilitate my work schedule and life in such a manner that he was in control of what I did and when I did it. He even arranged for me to tele-commute. I was not happy about this. I had been told I could work in the office so I could learn about Livorna and learn to do business the Livorna way. That was not the case. My home was 10 minutes from Livorna, and now Cal would have access to me at his leisure.

It was approximately a month after I began with the company that he actually raped me. He came over under the guise of installing the company software on my computer. He was in my chair, and he instructed me to sit near to observe the process. I was kneeling next to him and he lunged and took me to the floor and raped me. I pleaded for him to stop. He kept telling me that I should tell myself over and over, "I love Cal, I love Cal" and eventually I would love him and it would make all this "easier on me". Over the next 6 years I was Cal's puppet. Over time, I fell easily into the role I had grown up with. I was miserable, but that was an emotion I was all too familiar with. His control over me became more intrusive into my life as a single mother. I was a nervous wreck all the time that Cal would become angry with me for something and fire me. I did not have the self-esteem to stand up for myself. This was not familiar territory. I actually had my daughters trained to be quiet and hide under the view of the windows when Cal would come by. There were times that Cal would go into the back yard and tap on the windows and say "I know you are in there". We would stay quiet until he left. When he later would ask, I told him we had gone for a walk or across the street to a friend's home.

I had several moments when I saw that I was modeling for my girls a life and a behavior that was not healthy and that they were in danger of learning this behavior for themselves and allowing themselves to be manipulated in a manner like this, thinking it was the norm. I did nothing. I was frozen in my own fear and insecurities. I could tolerate the abuse so long as I could keep a roof over my girls' heads.

Then, after divorcing his wife, Cal had become emboldened. He was having inappropriate relations with other women at Livorna as well. I was grateful for this as it took some of the pressure off of me.

Then came the day that Cal made a strange demand. He wanted to buy his dream home and could not qualify for the loan based on his income alone. He told me I was to sign papers stating that my income was his income. I saw this as a direct danger to me keeping a roof over my daughters' heads. I declined and stated that I had just signed papers on my own home purchase. This angered him but what was done was done. Days later I went out and bought a home.

There was retaliation. Cal would give me negative write ups on cases; write ups that were clearly a warning that I had better step in line because he had the control of my job. These warnings and retaliations came often.

Cal was staying fairly busy with his other "girls," and one night I went to karaoke with a friend and met a man and brought him home with me. I told him all about Cal. He would become my protector. I told Cal I had a partner now and he would have to "let me go" and Cal was irate. That day he came to my home and raped me for the last time. I could not take it anymore. My heart, soul, and psyche were all broken beyond that which I could control. I had to make it stop.

I made a decision: I would commit suicide. I made a list of everything that I needed to do to accomplish this goal. On this list was change the beneficiary of my life insurance policy to reflect my longtime friend with the request that she take guardianship; write her a letter explaining why I did what I did and begging her to become a parent to my girls; write letters to Livorna staff members and management; find the right hotel in which to commit suicide; get a gun; buy Depends diapers. The diapers were needed to make sure I didn't make a mess. I was told the final act of our body is to empty the bowels and bladder. I had completed everything on my list except getting a gun. I planned to take one from my father's vast collection. When I realized that getting the gun was all I had left to do, it got real. I was starting to look at everyone with the thought that I hoped they would forgive me. That everyone would be better off. I would be better off, it would be over. No more abuse. Then, while praying, it came to me: I did not want to die; I just wanted "it" to stop.

I reached out for help. I called my doctor and told him what I had planned. After telling him I shelved the plan and opted for help. He put me in an intensive outpatient program (IOP). This program was one where I came to the facility 3 days a week, for 3 hours. It was a group therapy program. I learned that talking about what happened to me took away its power. I learned to love me. I learned to take care of me. Something as simple as positive and loving self-talk and a warm bubble bath are so important, healing and empowering. I also saw a specialist for PTSD. I found that with some medication to calm my anxieties, lots of talking, soul searching, and more talking, I had become strong and ready to call Joe at Livorna and ask for a private face to face away from the office.

Joe and I met at Denny's. I came armed with my truth and lots of e-mails to support my allegations. Joe listened to me; at times he looked as though he was going to be ill. Clearly Joe believed me. In confidence, he advised me to seek legal representation to protect myself. He then asked what I wanted. I told him I wanted Cal fired and I wanted to keep my job.

Well, I got half that wish. Cal was fired but I lost my job. The legal part of the matter was handled by attorneys. The company did their best to care for me. They extended my long term disability to the limits and beyond to allow me to take care of myself.

I took a very small settlement. During the litigation process, I had lived off credit cards. I was now able to pay those off. My greatest expense was the extended therapy for PTSD. I tell you, it was worth every penny. There is so much more to my life story that is me, and what brought me to this story. But through therapy and prayer, I have removed the "V" from my forehead. I am stronger! I have great self-esteem, confidence, and education (I got my GED). I made it! I am a survivor!

Looking back, I know I never wanted my life to end. I just needed help. Through my decision to reach out and ask for help I was able to stop the abuse. My life changed, but for the better. My world did not come to an end. My kids' world did not stop. If anything, they were empowered by seeing me stand up for myself.

If you have reached the point I was at, I want to say to you that suicide is a permanent solution to a temporary problem. Help is out there! All you have to do is reach out. I promise you, life IS good. It's really good. You are worth the effort!

Today, I am exactly where I am supposed to be. I am happy, fulfilled, joyful. I share my story with those who show interest. Part of my healing journey is to share with others what happened to me and how I made the decision to live. I hope my story inspires others in need to reach out.

Stay tuned for my solo book "Angel on My Shoulder" releasing later in 2018.

Finally, in all that I have experienced I had someone in my corner and I knew it. God! With God, no hurdle is too high!

Hugs & kisses,

Teresa Dye

*Not the real name of the person or company; randomly made up name.

Teresa Dye Biography:

Author~ Wife~ Mother~ Grandmother~ Survivor

Teresa Dye was born and raised in a potpourri of lower class suburbs of Sacramento, California by her alcoholic drug addicted mother and step father(s). Her biological father resided in Stanislaus County and was a larger than life ladies' man. She had two brothers, one older and one younger, and she was a homeless child of the streets for a period. She currently resides with her second husband in California's East Bay Area. Teresa was a single mother to two daughters now grown with children of their own; she a grandmother of six and great grandmother of two. She also has two step children. Now coming up on 57 years young she is retired from the commercial insurance industry and enjoys spending her time with her loved ones, including her golden retriever. She enjoys near daily visits to the gym, working with others in her community to keep litter off the streets and parks, painting ornaments, reading, writing, games, football (Go Raiders) and most of all, she enjoys her husband, who she believes is her soul mate, her destiny, the love of her life. After people get to know her and having heard of the challenges and triumphs of her life, Teresa has been told by a multitude of people that she needed to write a book. This chapter is her first foray to that end. Teresa credits God's grace for her survival mentally, physically and spiritually.

Tragedy to Triumph

By

Sequoia Moss

Age: 29

Pittsburg, CA

Nurse~Motivational Speaker~Holistic
Revivalist~Entrepreneur~Author

www.shalomtemplecare.com

Email: Sequoiamoss@gmail.com

Find me on Facebook, Instagram, Google+, and more!

You can't choose how your story begins, but you can change how you finish it. As for me, my story begins in the spring of 1988. I was born in Pittsburg, CA, at Los Medanos Community Hospital. I was four months old when I lost my father to the prison system. He was sentenced to seven years to life. As I grew older I learned my teenage mother had testified against my father and was forced to raise me on her own. I would later find out my mother suffered from mental illness. Growing up in a dysfunctional home hindered my personal growth. Witnessing physical and mental abuse became a regular occurrence for me; I experienced domestic violence, drugs, and sex early in life. My first experience with sexual trauma happened when I was seven years old. It was my own family member, and she continuously molested me. At the time I didn't understand it was a terrible thing, I only knew it was our secret. I believe through that experience, many gateways were unlocked that opened up to more trauma to haunt me for years to come. Molestation became a regular manifestation in my life: male family members would touch me, and I became a magnet for sexual energy and the presence was strong and heavy. As I transitioned into puberty the abuse at home became worse, and there was a shift in my attitude. I developed an "I don't care attitude" and I liked the attention I received, especially from older men. I desired to know what it felt like to be loved by someone. I felt like nobody loved me.

For me, life was tough, but I managed to get a job at 14 and was able to start taking care of myself. However, jealousy arose in my home, and arguments broke out about me helping with bills. As I became an independent teenager, I also became promiscuous, looking for love in all the wrong places. I began dating older men who didn't care how old I was. My home environment was toxic, and I was overloaded with chores and the responsibility to help raise my siblings. I didn't have the time or the energy for homework anymore. I was constantly subjected to trauma, such as having my menstrual products taken from me, my hair being cut off for being "too cute," being called ugly and dark, being hit in the eye, having blood vessels broken, and so much more. I found happiness nowhere. My social relationships suffered due to my choice of friends, and I felt attacked from every angle. I could not depend on myself for love. Everything I had suffered led me to attempt suicide, and all that got me was a 51/50 hold and my stomach pumped. After that experience, I promised I would never feel that low about myself or do that again.

One night when tension was high at home, I decided to lock myself in my room and just read. That was my favorite thing to do. I ignored the knocking because I knew what would happen. Suddenly, the police and EMS were at the door. My mom told them I tried to commit suicide again - and since I had done it before, they forced me to go with them. I couldn't believe this! For the next two weeks I had to go to a mental institution. Those two weeks turned into a month due to my mom and I not being able to come to an agreement on the medication I would take. Then, of course, I was finally sent back home. Things were fine for a couple weeks, but then they turned very bad. My mom decided to punish me by taking all my clothes and cutting them up. When I tried to stop her, she tried to stab me, and cut me in my abdomen! I was in shock, and at that point I had to fight for my life, because I really felt she was trying to kill me. We got into a physical tussle - and since she felt I got the best of her, she cut herself across her back and said she would tell the police I did it. The police believed her story, especially since she coached my siblings to support her lie. It wasn't their fault though, they were just young children. I spent a year in juvenile hall. The charges were lowered once they figured out my mom was lying. Then once again I was placed back home.

My mother put me out again. This was a regular thing, and she hid the part she played each time so well and I was always to blame. She would usually report me as a runaway right after. People were afraid to take me in because she would call the police on them, saying they were harboring a runaway. After sleeping in parks, cars and bushes, I was offered a hotel room by a man. I was unaware of the consequence that would come from receiving a warm bed and a hot meal. After getting the help I thought I needed, I was kidnapped by a pimp. I went missing for months, and to my surprise no one in my family reported me missing. When I got picked up by the police they saw a prostitute instead of a victim. The pimp came to the police station to get me, thinking I used the fake name he gave me, but I told my true name them, so I could get away. When I told the police how old I was they looked disappointed. I explained what happened to me, and the only thing he said was, "Why hasn't anyone reported you missing? You aren't even in our files as a runaway or anything." He had tears in his eyes and I was overwhelmed by emotions as well. I felt crushed; nobody loved me enough to believe the prior cries for help. No one loved me enough to look for me or even report me missing. From that point I wanted to change, but the anger from all the pain I had endured had taken hold of my heart. I was tarnished and trying to live "normally" was so hard. As a child I didn't understand the importance of rehabilitation and therapy, so as a damaged soul I tried at life again.

Foster homes, juvenile hall and group homes became my home. I constantly shifted from here to there. I knew better than to run away, so I complied and did as I was told. I was always told I wasn't a bad child, I was just misguided - but I couldn't believe that because I didn't like who I was. I realized I was being shaped by the system. I was around so many influences, good and bad. I ended up doing independent studies and graduated at age 17. On my 18th birthday I was given a garbage bag with all my clothes and personal belongings, since I had become too old for my group home and it was time for me to be a grown up. When I returned to Pittsburg, rumors of my life and relationship with my mother were everywhere. Nobody wanted to really deal with me, and I pushed away all the helping hands. I found myself back in the streets, selling everything possible, including my own body. I got into a relationship with a man who was no good for me. He became my pimp and beat me on a regular basis. I masked my pain with alcohol and drugs. I lost myself trying to be Bonnie to his Clyde. I would fight people, lie, cheat and steal. I knew I hurt so many people and encouraged them to partake in the horrible lifestyle I lived. In October 2009, my father wrote me a letter from prison. The letter hurt me because he said in so many words that he was giving up on me. He couldn't believe I had allowed myself to lose control of my life. I was so ashamed.

After reading the letter from my father, I knew I had to change. The problem was I didn't know how to - or what change looked like. I prayed on New Year's Eve 2009 asking for help, because I knew I was unable to do this on my own. The Most High blessed me with a change of mind and heart. The next day I left that toxic man, I applied for a job and I was hired. I applied for school and was accepted. Soon after, I met the man who would become my husband. I knew it was nothing but The Most High blessing me. I began going to church and reading my Bible. I didn't have a strong church background; we were what you call CEO (Christmas & Easter Only) church goers. I visited several churches searching for a church home. During this transition in my life, I got married and we started our family. I had two daughters with my husband and did the best I could, but the pain of my past was starting to rise and spill into my marriage. I still had healing I needed in my life. Issues with my mother arose again. She would call CPS (Child Protective Services) on me, making false reports, calling my job and my husband to tell them I used to be a prostitute. She even went as far as calling my husband's job trying to get him fired. Although my mother hurt me in so many ways, I just really wanted a relationship with her. I wanted to forgive her but didn't understand that sometimes forgiveness requires cutting ties. I learned forgiveness was a huge part of my healing.

When a person doesn't deal with their past, it will always resurface. One terrible experience after the next caused me to almost lose my marriage and my sanity. Old behaviors arose and when I had depleted myself I FINALLY surrendered to God. I would attend church, but I kept leaving empty. I stepped out of church to build a personal, spiritual relationship with God. I began studying my Bible and biblical Hebrew. During this time, I was reunited with my husband. Within my Hebrew studies I learned to call God "YAH," and YAH began to bless my life with an abundance of information, allowing me to engage with many like-minded people. I gave birth to our first son in 2015 and many more blessings began raining on me. My father was released from prison after almost 28 years. A stranger paid my debts to go back to school. I began taking college courses to learn more. I started connecting to my African roots and holistic spirituality. I received a vision of my purpose: to help women connect back to nature as well as one another by embracing sisterhood. To complete the first step, I had to complete nursing school. My amazing husband paid for me to accomplish my goal. I experienced many trials during the time I was in school, but my faith was even greater. YAH allowed me to shine through tribulation. I graduated with great honors and launched the business YAH had presented me with. At this chapter in my life I am continuing my education to extend my business to the healthcare industry. I'm taking it one goal at a time. My business, Shalom Temple Care, is a piece of my heart I want to give back to the world. My blog reflects my journey into being spiritually reborn.

There was still one component missing in my life. I had all this knowledge on health, on biblical history, and education, but when I left the church I left fellowship. My walk became depressing and overwhelming. I lost my zeal looking for YAH in books, not realizing YAH is in me. I recently had a divine intervention, and I began to understand the importance of fellowship, realizing that fellowship is required to be held accountable - one aspect of my life I missed out on for the last three years walking in what most call truth. Yes, I had gotten better in life, yes, I received blessings, but I needed accountability so others would keep me liable and responsible when I did things wrong. Walking alone in this spiritual journey, I did not have anyone to correct me so I could be reproved. I knew this was important and would eventually help me to reflect and become a better person, especially with my mission to help others.

Through faith and obedience, I have been granted a holy sisterhood that is biblically based. I have sisters all over the world I speak to. Having sisters just as hungry as you are to please The Most High is beautiful and powerful. I have been granted mother figures that love on me and pour into me. I learned a mother isn't just a title, but also requires actions of love. There was a time the title "mother" held such power over me. I allowed myself to suffer inexcusable abuse as an adult, just to hold on to a person who held a title. Being a mother now I couldn't imagine hurting my children. I just cry thinking of how much I love them. They keep me grounded. I had to make a decision as a mother to protect my children by first protecting myself. They watch my every move and I don't ever want them to allow someone who doesn't see their value have any relevance or influence in their lives. Never stay around people who hurt you intentionally no matter what title they hold. It is unhealthy and toxic. In actuality, I realized what we accept from others is a reflection of what we think we deserve. I had to lead by example and sever the roots to dysfunction. I have found Shalom (completeness and peace) in my life. I have been restored. I have cut ties with everyone who meant to cause me pain, no matter who they are. Today I can say I love myself and who I am. I can only thank YAH for allowing me to see clearly and walk with so much resilience. Being able to look back and know that my past doesn't make me, it didn't break me. I may have fallen only to get back up and stand taller than before. Healing is a journey, it doesn't happen overnight.

One thing I do have to share is the first thing I have had to do to begin my healing process. The first step in my process was to forgive myself for the survival instincts I acquired in that time of my life. The next step was to appreciate the opportunity to become better daily. My spiritual advice does not limit anyone; no matter what religion a person stems from, I believe connecting back to nature and to who you are is essential to receive complete wholeness. I have been chosen to be a light by our Higher Power. I know that my testimony will help many who are going through traumatic experiences in their lives. There are many things we endure that help shape who we are and what life means to us. After telling my story, the main thing I want people to learn is that they are not alone and are truly loved by The Creator of All Things. I am in the process of writing my own solo book. I have come across remarkable women with similar backgrounds, and due to many reason they don't have a voice or an advocate. Many women face these battles alone and face judgement by others who just don't understand. I am bringing back women's healing circles. It's my goal to inspire other to take the first step toward their healing journey.

Sequoia Moss Biography:

Nurse~Motivational Speaker~Holistic
Revivalist~Entrepreneur~Author

Sequoia Moss was born in the East Bay Area Pittsburg, CA. Adversary found her at an early age, losing her father to the prison systems at 4 months old and being raised by a mentally ill teenage mother. Physical and mental abuse, molestation and heartbreak was prevalent in her life. Sequoia went on a roller coaster of catastrophes that landed her in foster homes, juvenile hall and group homes, eventually landing her in the hands of a pimp at age 16. Drugs, prostitution and domestic violence followed her into adulthood. She has fought an uphill battle searching for The Most High. Many mistakes and self-inflicted trauma caused her to surrender her life to YAH (God). Divine intervention has brought her spirit back in the hands of YAH. She has learned to value being transparent and her mission is to share her journey to inspire others. Sequoia is a wife to a loving, supportive husband and her union has been blessed with 3 beautiful children. She is a licensed cosmetologist, certified phlebotomist and recent nursing school graduate. She runs a small home business, Shalom Temple Care, that brings awareness to taking care of your temple (your body) and restoring spiritual and holistic culture to women. She realizes the importance of self-love and sisterhood and strives to revive what has been lost. Sequoia's story is to restore faith and for others to see that darkness isn't your final destination in life.

When Love Was No Longer Enough

By

Danae Braggs

Real Estate Agent ~Author ~ Entrepreneur ~ Speaker & All Around Superwoman

Pittsburg, CA Native

Business Cell: 925-329-8825

From parent to child and child to parent there's an expected organic love and bond. Sometimes that bond is unbalanced on either side, leaving the one who loves more to long for more love in return.

Normally, a ride to Oakland on a cool June Saturday morning would mean a great day, but not this cool June Saturday morning. The final destination of this freeway ride would forever change my life. We were not on our way to my favorite aunt's house. We were not on our way to do any shopping. We weren't even on our way to church.

We were on our way to an "appointment". My mother, my older sister and I were riding silently up Highway 4, making our way off the 680 to the 24 and through the Caldecott Tunnel. I rolled my window down some and let the fresh morning air blow on my face as I ate a cracker despite being warned not to eat or drink anything after midnight the night before. At that moment my mind shut off. I was now on auto-pilot. Yes, this was that appointment.

We pulled up to a parking lot. This place was seemingly busy for an early Saturday morning. The building was tall, drab and grey with lots of windows looking down like sad eyes. Inside it seemed like a cattle call. I thought to myself, "Is everyone's appointment today?"

If you haven't already guessed, yes, this is an abortion clinic. I was 15 years old and at the end of my freshman year in high school. The night before this appointment I suddenly realized that contrary to everything I was taught, my body was not my own. I was stripped of the right to choose what happened to and within my body. A choice was made for me. Who knows what thought process was used to get to the actual decision, but the explanation I was given didn't give me any inclination that this decision was made with me or my future in mind. Not because I was smart. Not because I was beautiful. Not because I had all the potential in the world. Not because I was going to be somebody. There was only one reason given: I was told that I was not going to "embarrass" someone. This reason had nothing to do with me. What my body, mind and spirit were about to experience had absolutely NOTHING to do with me. On the surface and given the explanation, it had everything to do with how someone else thought others would think of them. Apparently, having a pregnant 15 year old daughter in 1994 was embarrassing. Hearing those words made me feel like nothing.

All the way from Pittsburg to Oakland that next morning I felt empty. I didn't care if I died on that table. I actually hoped I would. Maybe it would hurt them the way they hurt me. I hated my dad, I hated my mom and I hated my sister. I even hated myself.

As we were waiting my mother told me, "You'll feel better when it's over." Uggggh! How could she possibly know? Why would I feel better about something I didn't want to do in the first place? This is something she often said to get me to do something that I was hesitant to do. All I could do is roll my eyes. Then a nurse called me back. The doctor checked me out and then asked me several questions; not sure what my auto-pilot answers were. Neither the questions nor the answers mattered. I was already there wearing a stupid hospital gown being prepped for the one of the worst things that could happen to me. The only question I remember him asking was "Have you eaten anything after midnight?" I wanted to tell him no, let them put me to sleep and hope I didn't wake up. I didn't. I told him that I had eaten a cracker and a couple of gummie worms that morning. The doctor responded, saying that they wouldn't be able to put me to sleep and I would probably feel what was happening. GREAT! Talk about adding insult to injury.

After it was all over, my mom and my sister thought it would be a great idea to go shopping, as if I felt like walking through a shopping center. At that point I didn't even care what hurt. I was a zombie. For the rest of that day I was a full-fledged zombie. Not from any medication or even shock; a piece of my heart and soul was just suctioned from my body along with my unborn child. I didn't care about anything at that point. I truly believe this was the very first time I realized that love was no longer enough. It wasn't enough that I loved my parents. It wasn't enough that I loved that baby. It wasn't even enough that I kind of loved myself. This situation, like many others, required more than love: It required strength, compassion and sensitivity. At this point in my life love was no longer enough. As a matter of fact, from that moment love was not even a factor in my life anymore. It would take a long time for me to realize how this one moment in time truly impacted my life, especially in future relationships.

Going forward, I taught myself to guard my heart. My heart no longer really had anything to do with the decisions I made except for what I did to protect it. Love was buried down deep in a wound sealed with spite and hatred. The spite I carried determined my motives and the hatred in my heart made me act on them.

Some time went by and my sister apologized for her part in the ordeal. My parents, on the other hand, have yet to mention a word of this incident since the night before it happened. This ultimately created another link in the chain of events that would change my entire life. I decided that nobody but me would control what I did with my body going forward.

Around October 1994, I found out that I was pregnant. I didn't say a word to anyone but my boyfriend. Who was going to even notice? My parents were preoccupied with whatever they had going on and I didn't feel safe enough or comfortable enough to share that information at that time with them or anyone else. I was traumatized by what happened before and it wouldn't happen again! I didn't hide anything. No one noticed. I can say that I never got really big, so I guess that helped. It wasn't a secret because I was embarrassed; it was because I refused to have something else taken from me. I protected my heart and my baby with my silence.

In January 1995, I turned 16 years old. In March, the cat was out of the bag and on May 26th 1995, by way of an unnecessary C-Section, I had a baby girl. Jasmine Danae. The moment she was born love was again enough, but not for everyone. I still felt the same way I had before but my heart opened up for her. Now I had to finish something else I started. I was a GATE Student (Gifted and Talented Education), read at college level in the 3rd grade, got straight A's (when I wanted to), a computer genius, etc. It made no sense to not finish school no matter what the spite in my heart said. My mind was intelligent enough to know that stopping there would only hurt me. I refused to be a statistic.

Going into my junior year that fall, I decided to complete the credits I missed due to missing the end of the previous school year as well as the credits necessary for junior year and senior year all at the same time. I did that! This would lead to more overachiever accomplishments.

Throughout the 24 years since that fateful day, my relationships have been determined by the way the love in my heart was set up. Ups and downs were as common as loops on a roller coaster, my relationship with my parents included. In more recent years I have opened up about this with my younger sister who had no idea it even happened. Needless to say, she was appalled. My relationship with my parents has since repaired, although that day has still not been discussed. I can say that incident did help me sharpen the tools I would need to endure some even harder situations that include infidelity, financial ruin, severe depression and even suicide attempts, just to name a few.

In this life we come to a point where we have to realize love is not enough. We need compassion, empathy, reciprocation, understanding, etc. There are many ingredients to this recipe we call "living" and all are needed to survive. We spend time looking for the missing pieces to our wholeness but a lot of times we miss what is right in front of us directing us to the next stepping stone on our life path. In order to move forward we have to look back and find the clues as to why we are what and who we are in this very moment. Once we have that information, it's up to us to make adjustments and live our best life.

Danae Braggs Biography:

Real Estate Agent ~Author ~ Entrepreneur ~ Speaker & All
Around Superwoman

A Pittsburg, CA native, Danae Braggs is an all-around
SUPERWOMAN. Becoming a mother at 16, she had every
reason to also become a statistic. She never did. She soared
above the odds and surpassed a lot of lackluster
expectations. Today she is a successful entrepreneur, real
estate agent, and author; just to name a few of her many
accomplishments. Her philanthropic endeavors almost always
promote her beloved city, Pittsburg. She is also the secretary
of Branches of Community Services, a local non-profit
focused on giving back to our youth and our community. She
is also a featured author in *Breaking Through Barriers Volume
1 & 2 and Broken Into Brilliance Volume 1 & 2,* making her a 5
time author. She has been quoted as saying "I'm from here
from here..." An advocate for children, housing rights, self-
sufficiency and more, Danae shows and proves that she is the
epitome of the term SUPERWOMAN.

Closing Chapter

(Healing & Forgiveness)

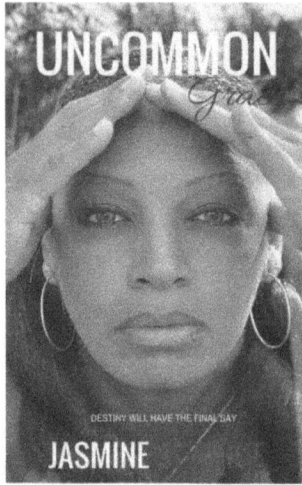

Chance of a Lifetime

By

Jasmine Strange

Author~ Award-Winning Singer~ Mother~ Model

strangefundamentals@yahoo.com

A second chance is not always given, nor has it been found to be a standard practice in life itself. When one receives a gift as precious as such, healing is in motion and forgiveness a must.

It was a night of honor, a night of fun, a night to remember, a night well done. I stood upon a brightly lit stage at the historic California Theatre in Pittsburg; a stage once graced by the presence of many of the world's top performers. I would not only sing that night but also receive an award that evening from a local community organization (9QUOTA). The award was for Gospel Artist of the Year! I felt full of life and on top of the world. With each bat of my eye, glitter, shown sparkling on my face would catch my mother's eye. She came! Though late at night on a chilly evening in January, my mom, battling flu-like symptoms, said she wouldn't have missed it for the world. This was, in fact, the town in which my mother was born and raised back when there was a hospital in it. This was a theatre that many a famous person passed through when they came to town to perform. It was a grand ol' event I will never forget.

I would be ministering in song; a piece I wrote in reference to how short this life can be, how you can be here one day and gone the next. I wrote it for a friend of mine who lost his 17 year old son in the blink of an eye to an asthma attack just after his high school graduation. This night, I'd preface my song by asking the audience members to look to the left and the right of them, and to think of their loved ones at home. "Love on those family members and friends that are here with us", I said, "as you never know what day could be your last." I shared with them how rough my year had been but how absolutely irrelevant that was in the greater scheme of things, as what's most important is that I have loved ones here that I can still hold and call with the added comfort of hearing their voice. A murmur of agreement filled the theatre as the statement hit home for quite a few. I let them know that amongst those people I cherished the most were my friends in the audience, my children, Lyric and Cadence, and my beautiful mother Mrs. Stingily. As I pointed to her in the audience, a roar of applause could be heard from the building, as I am sure she had gained much love and respect having been an educator in that community for many years. Chills ran up my arms as we all shared a moment in time. I picked up the microphone and sang with one of my largest and most longtime supporters in the house, MOM. That would be the last time I'd see my mother's eyes open for 7 straight days.

I sat motionless facing the window, head thrown back toward the heavens, unable to hold back the tears streaming from the corners of my eyes. Squeezing my lids tight I pressed my fake eyelashes against the tops of my cheeks. I could feel the glue in them begin to loosen from the moisture created by the continuous flow of tears. My lashes, which had held on since the show, began to lift from the corners, giving me the appearance of an inebriated Mrs. Piggy…no no wait… more like Snuffleupagus in a wind storm…but I didn't care. My world had frozen for but a moment in time. In the slowest of motion, I placed my hands on top of my head and began to ponder not only the physical space I was in but the mental space that accompanied it. Where do I go from here? What is my role in all of this? What really is my true purpose? What will my tomorrow hold? My next hour, minutes and seconds would hang in the balance and rest in the hands of the Good Lord. Was it my fault that she was out that late in the cold to watch me sing??? Had I done all I could do leading up to this point to have kept her from this state? Should I have known this was coming, signs and all? How badly had I failed? Would I get the opportunity to correct my steps? Or, was it too late~ and would I be forgiven if it so?

Life is a gift and the amount of time in it an added bonus. How do we show our thanks and appreciation for the greatest gift there is? Have we stopped long enough in this busy plight of existence we call living to truly cherish the air that fills our lungs, the experiences we've been given, or the loved ones that have shared it with us along the way? What if today was your last? Have you had the chance to say "I am sorry" or "I apologize for..."? Have you had the opportunity to exercise forgiveness to those in need of it? Perhaps, the person who needs your forgiveness most is yourself?

A long beep would sound and snap me out of my self-induced zone. It was one of the many sounds happening simultaneously amongst multiple machines functioning independently, yet together as a well-oiled conduit, an immulant of vitality. Monitored above our heads were blood pressure, heart rate, oxygen levels, life support, catheter readings, picc lines, art lines, medicine and nutrient IV's, etc. How absolutely fascinating it was to witness all of this man made machinery operating as one for the greater cause of a purpose. Why can't we make ourselves to do the same, I wondered. What are we missing here? What can be learned from such a thing??? As an educator, I believe every moment in time is an opportunity for a lesson to be learned.

My mother lay motionless in a hospital bed located on the second floor. Above the doorway entrance read the letters I. C. U. We had somehow arrived in the intensive care unit. Fighting for her life, my mother's chest would rise up and down in an artificial rhythmic motion in accordance to the life support machine that was actually doing the work for her, as her lungs had collapsed leaving her breathless. Here she would lay for what seemed an eternity. Helpless, I stood, paced, sat and stood again for hours upon hours and days upon days. Thoughts raced in my head of my childhood: Was I a good enough daughter? Where did our relationship go south? How would I ever be able to mend it now? Why hadn't I taken the time to detect the signs leading up to this occurrence?

I will never say I know what it feels like to have a parent that has gone on to glory, but for sure I was getting the smallest taste of it as days 1, 2,3 and 4 had passed without a wink from her. Inundated with questions, scenarios and demands from doctors, nurses and family that I just couldn't conceive or even process at the time, I'd soon be asked to sign papers and make decisions that I just wasn't prepared for. Oh God! What was going on? My head was spinning. My body was hot.

My thoughts were muddled. Days 5 and 6 would approach…each with the anticipation of seeing her eyes again and hearing her voice, all to no avail and only to be told, "I'm sorry ma'am today will not be the day, but perhaps tomorrow?" I had never felt so empty in my life, so scared, so sick to my stomach and with such desire for a second chance.

Day 7 would present its face, as the sun arose yet again, only this day would be different. This day would be a gift like every other day was but with a special type of wrapping paper. The gift of authentic life would be delivered on this day as my mother's intubated state would soon be extubated!

Her body, though not awake, had been working overtime fighting to heal. So on this 7th day her rest would begin. "And on the 7th day, He rested." This, a paraphrased version from Genesis in the Bible came to mind. The doctor came in bright and early and loudly called out my mother's name. Her eyes popped open and she began to answer his questions, of course by way of a nod and obediently following the commands and requests to squeeze his hand or wiggle her toes. This day he would look over to me and smile… a reassurance that everything was going to be alright. Realize that this was a complete collective and shared sigh of relief for everyone in the room, as the days prior the doctor could barely look me in the face as if to say, "I really don't know what the outcome will be and unfortunately, I can't at this time give you any sense of hope."

In my head, the doctor and I were holding hands while jumping up and down; he due to a complete satisfaction in the accomplishment of his life's work, and me that he had hung in there long enough to allow God to save my mama. My mother looked at him and over to me then back at him again and smiled, even with her mouth full of tubes and cords. She didn't know quite what was going on but she knew enough to know that something pretty special had just taken place. We were all the recipient of this priceless miracle on that day and oh what a gift it was!

Excitement filled the room as we all kind of ~ sort of "GOT IT." This is what life is all about. This is what teamwork is all about. This is what can be acquired when you have a common goal and work together toward it. Because of the collective effort of all involved, the buzzer had not gone off as of yet...the game was not over! This was but a mere half time. This was a chance to get "IT" right or die trying, as they say.

As my mother came to, we realized as happy as we were, It would be a long road to a full recovery, one which we welcomed with open arms of course but one that required great heart, courage, hard work, planning and strategy. That was merely a saved life. Now, healing must begin and the fight toward living takes place. This too would take a team effort. Some would have to step up in this part of the game and others would step back. It is the natural process of life. Role reversals and changes of the guard would soon follow. Awkward…

In the days to follow I had so much to say, as did my mother. I was so determined and ready to fix my lips to tell ALL. I wanted to tell my mama everything! I wanted to pull my child card and run to mama with all of my problems and issues that I had acquired just by her being in there. I wanted to tell her what was said to me during that time period and just how it made me feel….none of which mattered, none of which was needed nor would help in moving forward in a healthy healing effort of motion. Remember, I thought to myself, that was yesterday. Today is a new day! Cliché as it sounds, I "got it" for the first time. Today was a new day and I was steady walking into yesterday.

Speaking of walking, my mom could not, little did she know. As far as she knew, this time lapse could have easily been 10 minutes to an hour, possibly a whole day. To her surprise and upon asking me her first question of how long she had been in there, I informed her it had in fact been 7 days. She hadn't moved in 7 days: not an eyelash, not a twitch. Have you ever not moved in a 24 hour period of time let alone 24 times 7? On my most depressed of days, I may have slept for a 24 hour period but rest assured I rolled over, wiped tears from my eyes, blew my nose and most definitely walked to the restroom. Indeed, I was moving, but 7 DAYS supine??? Just as I had my ideas of all I was going to tell her, she had hers in that same moment. Neither of us were fully prepared to actually receive the information necessary from the other in that exact moment to help in that forward forgiving motion of healing. Knowledge is necessary before any act is ever successfully achieved or carried out. Thus, we wrestled a bit in this arena.

Her next question was, "What is today's date?, to which she responded, upon receipt of her answer, " Well...I have a letter of recommendation due!" Wow! How could she know that? Her wherewithal was clearly intact in the mind even if not yet in the body. Therefore, I was quickly checked by my mother after attempting to tell her about my experience while she was out. I wanted to tell her how hurt I was and how violated I felt. She said, "Jasmine, you can't worry about that right now. You have to forgive them." Huh??? I was so angry. I was so hurt by the way things took place and unfolded, both within my control and circumstances that were not. I wanted her to side with me. She didn't. She wasn't against me mind you...just making me aware of what was most important and "what" was not. We had been given a second chance at life and I was stuck on what promotes death and not that that promotes healing and life. She said, as she has often told me before, "Jasmine, you have to throw that off of you. You must forgive in order to heal. Holding on to those Ill thoughts will make you sick." A flood of light bulb emojis surrounded my head in that moment!!!!!! WHOA! I had totally missed the mark.

We have difficulties in healing often times because we are continually fighting against the very essence of what helps us to move forward. In life, we use the verb walk as an expression of a means or mode of transportation propelling us from one place, one state or one realm to another. Ironically, it is our "heels" that support us as we push off to advance moment by moment and year to year. The definition of a human heel reads: the back part of the human foot; the part of a shoe that SUPPORTS the heel. Support is definitely what we need in times of "healing," isn't it? Take for instance a boat; a boat "heeling" would be a boat being tilted temporarily by pressure or wind, or by an uneven distribution of weight aboard. When life gets rocky, filled with pressure and throws us off balance we tend to shift and lean back on our "heels" temporarily, as that is what sustains us and gives us the support necessary to push off again into a straightened, uplifted and forward motion. Clearly, my mother was speaking through me at this moment with these word plays of character and rhetorical excursions and double entendres.

I couldn't help but to research the two meanings of the words heal and heel just to locate the uncanny similarities of their importance. One of the words is located beneath and behind you in typical support positions and the other inside out...neither are in places of great view to the naked eye while in motion but both play a crucial part in relationship to insuring your well-being. The largest connection I found between the two were that heel and heal share the common goal of restoration. Both are in place to support you while aiding you to return toward your original functioning state.

On that note, it would appear that to heal is an indication of moving forward. A baby lays, then rolls , then crawls, then stands, in that order, prior to walking and eventually runs. When you have an accident or wind up in a position or situation such as my mother did and end up supine, on your back, for 7 motionless days straight, best believe you do not wake up running! The hardest part of passing out and waking up 7 days later is that your mind is no longer in sync with your body. As I mentioned, my mother's mind was sharp as a tack. She was blessed indeed, although there is a healing that must first take place in the mind prior to even that of the body.

When I mentioned earlier that a change in guard would take place at some point that could be awkward....well...here we were. You see, when she fell asleep, she was the mother/ the adult. She thought for herself, went where she pleased and made her own decisions. She was actually driving and removed from the car by ambulance the night they arrived. On the other side of waking up, she was now the baby and quite angry about it! She had no muscle memory activated, as the doctor would come to tell us that for every day you are motionless you digress 3 to 4 days and will need to rehabilitate to get back to base line. 7 days was only the period of time in which it took my mother to awake. She was still in the hospital bed in the ICU for another 7 and now in a rehabilitation/nursing facility for the last several weeks. The first week she was bed ridden as well. Therefore, we are looking at about 20 days' time 3 lost days, each equaling just over 60 days of relearning everything she once knew and did before she went out. So, you drove before you woke up? You now cannot. You ate and dressed yourself? You now cannot. You held the phone to your own ear and walked to the bathroom??? You now CANNOT! Imagine waking up to someone feeding you and wiping your backside? These have been the most humiliating days I can imagine of my mother's life. One day you are a college professor enjoying a night out at the theatre watching your daughter perform, and the next day food is falling all over your chest from missing your lips due to a lack of not only hand eye coordination but also lacking the muscle to perform such a simple task. Imagine people speaking over you to others as if you were not even there.

I tried to be there for my mom every day. I wanted to be a "good daughter", but I found it to be a daunting task as she was now the baby and I the mom. Truly, I wasn't ready. It was like having a baby with colic on some days and a toddler in the terrible two's on others who refused every bit of help you offered because they wanted to do it on their own although you knew good and well they couldn't. I'd lift the fork to her mouth in an attempt to feed her. She would try to slap it away, turning her head in the opposite direction. She wouldn't eat if she couldn't do it by herself and often times spilled food all over her chest when she did. Something as simple as raising her hand to her chest was like me lifting an elephant to the sky, and not only not being able to lift that elephant but not even making the target of something as large as the sky.

"I am not a baby!" she would announce. "Oh but you are", the doctor would reply, angering her even the more. "Our goal is to get you to the toddler stage." She blankly stared into space as if to be trapped like Alice in Wonderland where nobody understands you. Literally she dropped down the rabbit hole and was a completely different size overnight with the inability to function in the world in which she was accustomed before falling asleep. I won't even pretend to understand how disoriented that would feel to me.

Prior to landing in this recovery facility, she awoke in the initial receiving hospital, as I mentioned, stating, "This is not the hospital I asked to go to." All of us, ambulance drivers, emergency responders, my aunts, myself, nurses and the doctors in charge could only hope for her forgiveness, as this was the best decision we could make at the time and in the amount of time we had to save her life. Like me, in the beginning, she refused to lean on the HEEL necessary to HEAL. She had to learn to forgive the circumstances and welcome the process; forgive the circumstance and move forward to the new beginning she had been given no matter where she was or how she had gotten there. She was alive! It is truly a "NEW OUTLOOK ON LIFE". How you see how the world from one day to the next can determine your progress or detriment. There comes a point in life when we are shut down, cut down, and sometimes even burned down to the ground in order to receive the rejuvenation of a new life. We can look at it as a curse or a blessing or refuse to look at it at all and live a bitter unhealthy life to the end. Thank God for choices! Thank God for grace. Thank God for the ability to finish this race. Let's all look deep within, cut to the core, and cry out to LIVE AGAIN!

Immediately after refusing her food, my mother would ask to go to the bathroom. They offered her a bed pan. She refused, saying, "I can walk to the bathroom by myself!" When they told her she could not she was infuriated as that was the last thing she wanted to hear. She began to try. Tears surfaced again in the corners of my eyes and hers as well. It was hard to watch a woman with the strength of an ox, the wit of a fox and a will just shy of God, succumb to a conditional state where all functions were temporarily locked. Her arms began to shake as sweat beads fell from her pain-stricken face, a shade of red that I couldn't erase. She fell backwards into her bed. The initial bathroom attempt had failed. The realization set in that yesterday was no longer, but a chance at tomorrow had been given. As difficult as it was she forgave the circumstances, forgave those that she felt were in the way of her progress and, most of all, forgave herself. Humbled would be the word I'd choose to represent her in that moment.

I remembered having a similar humbling moment when I tore my ACL during a collegiate basketball game. My opponent pushed me as I was going up for a lay-up! I landed on unbalanced footing, tearing my anterior cruciate ligament away from the bone in my knee. I lost control of my leg and slammed into the bleachers. I got up, hobbling, and I fought tooth and nail to get back into the game, claiming and convincing my trainers and coaches of my ability to do so. I subbed back in as they adhered to my stubborn demands only to fall flat on my face! What would happen next would be out of my control. This is sometimes how life is. As much as we desire the control, it is not always in our possession. I would soon be replaced for a season and my starting role given to the next player in line. I had to sit back and focus on what I could control and that was my will to heal. I had to worry less about being a good basketball player and more about what it would take to be a good patient. "OUCH!"

I found myself in a situation that I alone could not fix. I needed professional physical and emotional support and had to submit my pride, not my dignity, but my pride to those who were professionally skilled to get me back to where I needed to be. I did just that. Due to my injury, I was unable to try out for the professional women's league that had just come out but later played in the Pro-Am. I subsequently became Head Coach of Loyola University's women's basketball program. God had another direction for me to go. I don't regret it. I am thankful for where it has carried me both professionally and personally. There is something to say about a dose of humility. Oh, and I forgave the player that caused my injury. After all; she helped in the process of who I have become today and I live to write about it! Everything happens for a reason, as my son often reminds me.

Day by day my mother would heal and exercise forgiveness to the 10th power. She was eventually moved to a private room where the sun appeared in full view each morning a reminder of the Son who is life himself. The flowers bloom in her very presence, bringing the aroma of new life, the gift of seeing the deer that come to greet her at her window represent the family and friends that visit her around the clock. This was a sign of life in itself. She has humbled herself to allow the occupational and physical therapists to help her. She could now get up on her own and used the walker to get to the bathroom, a feat she struggled to achieve yet conquered all in preparation to walk home to her new life, something her former roommate couldn't do as she had no legs and was now preparing for hospice. A walk into her next life would be a walk into her heavenly home.

Before you walk home, can you find it in your heart to forgive your earthly circumstances enough to receive the gift of healing, a second chance that many don't get? I don't know where you are in your life. I don't know what you have lost or what may have recently been altered: your marriage, mate, job, child, spot on the team, an injury perhaps, but I challenge you to stop in this very moment. Re-evaluate the life that has been set before you. Forgive those that trespass against you. Forgive those who have tried to help you and maybe didn't know just how to effectively do so. Forgive your circumstances and what got you there in the first place. Forgive yourself. Thank God from whence you have come. Thank Him for where He is taking you. Be blessed in this very moment for the gift of a second chance at life! Be humbled by your experience and get excited while strategically planning your road toward the process of healing.

Everything living was designed to grow in an upward, forward or outward motion; expansion, that is. If you are living, you should be growing. When we stop growing we cease to live. Brokenness is a part of life and the struggle to overcome it an equal part. Your struggle is not a forever moment but an instrumental time in space that builds the strength needed to climb to your next destination, hence the butterfly. The need to heal is not a weakness but an opportunity to grab on to a power higher than your own, giving you a chance at a supernatural experience. It is those who refuse to lean on their heel (help from a friend, doctor, therapist, professional guidance field workers, mom, dad, family, GOD...) that ultimately prolong or sabotage their healthiest outcomes possible. Tear down that outer rocky layer today and let someone in. Someone is counting on your healing to break them through. That's just how it works; a law of the kingdom. Don't quote me...it just sounded good.

My mom is being released this week as I type! It is your turn to be released! If you are reading this, YOU have been given another chance to heal and another chance to forgive. Though it is not always an easy road forward, it is a necessary one; a rewarding one and one that is not promised to everyone. You, my friend, are the blessed one. Forgive and begin to heal today! With all of the love in my heart ~ Jaz

Jasmine Strange Biography:

Author~ Award-Winning Singer~ Mother~ Model

Jasmine was born in Oakland California and raised between California and Illinois. Lover of the Lord, this woman of God touches the hearts of man by lending herself back unto His hands to do His mighty works here on earth day in and day out. Finding one's life purpose is her mission as she walks in the world gracefully guided by the hand of the master.

She is a 44 year old single mother of two successful musicians, Lyric Fox of Howard University's Show Band and Cadence Strange of Pacific Boy Choir Academy/Oakland Symphony; graduate of the University of Illinois; author of the book "Uncommon Grace", independent recording artist and song writer; two time 9QUOTA Gospel Artist of the Year recipient; 2018 Bay Area Gospel Award nominee for Up and Coming Artist of the Year. Jasmine Strange currently sings with the Oakland Symphony and she is a member of the singing group Judah. She is a professional and certified educator of over 20 years and has received Teacher of the Year recognition at two of her teaching locations, Illinois and California. Vice President of her police academy class, she's a former police officer and received a leadership award from the Mayor of Bellwood, Illinois where she served. Amongst all else, Jasmine has an athletic side to her. She formerly played women's basketball for the University of Illinois and was captain of her squad before becoming the youngest head coach on the (MCC) Mid-West Collegiate Conference as Head Coach of the NCAA Women's Basketball Program at Loyola University; Jasmine has now taken the direction of public speaking and life coaching. She aspires to inspire the world by not only modeling in photos, yet another career of hers, but also by modeling the walk of Christ and the principles which God has set for us to use to improve the wholeness of our lives here on earth. She has since founded the organization G.I.G.G.L.E., Girls' In God's Grace Laugh Eternally, striving to restore the joy back into the lives of our youth.

Jasmine is currently under the leadership of Bishop Carl C. Smith at New Destiny Church, Pittsburg, California where she sings on the praise team with True Worship. She was the vocal director and praise and worship leader at Seed of Faith and directed the youth choir during her stint with the ministry. She has both hosted music workshops and spoken at various music workshops. Her charismatic personality and vocal gifts landed her positions such as vocal director for several plays, the latest being the WIZ (CCC) Theatre as well as a major acting/vocal role in the world premiere of Xtigone written by Nambi E. Kelly (African American Theatre Company).

FROM DEEP WITHIN

BY

JASMINE STRANGE

From deep within my soul cries
My freedom trapped down deep inside
Smothered, covered by the turbulence of life
Choked out by defeat lost love and strife
Lungs constricted, heart conflicted
Barely breathing….all but con-de-ceiving
A kind of debilitative mindset….idiosyncratic

You see, for years I've suffered in silence and pain
And for years I've suffered for others to gain
For years I've lived through the guilt…through the shame,
Through the fears of life, through the heartaches that came

I've plowed through some storms n' I've run through the rain
Even lost my direction, no longer IN FRAME
Now, try to focus on that! A target untrained
No form of guidance
A will with no aim

Stomach in knots tryna' play this game that had no rules…
Just bullies and wolves with deceptive hooves
You'll lose every time when the game's played with fools!
See, it's called Russian Roulette when you let the devil bet
On a life that's predestined now a pre-mature upset

But my mother once told me don't cry when milk spills
Just…clean it up…cuz the slip is what kills
Your life's worth much more…
Much more than a fall
Just look to the hills cuz the blood covers all

So stand tall….face the stall… GET READY GET SET!
The gun shoots a warning you'll never forget
A release from your soul says it's time to PRO-JECT
The courage you'll need to make the devil sweat
It's a courage that links your past to your future
Your now is the glue, your surgery suture
So dig deep my sistas, WITHIN dig deep!
Cut, uncover and EXPOSE what is sleep

Surgery may be needed just to cut away
The dysfunction that keeps us from a brighter day!
So scream to the heavens… I W A N T T O L I V E!
Then surrender on your knees and say Father I give!!!
Take my heart, take my soul, Father inject
Strength n' confidence
While you lead and protect
Then wisdom will come as I sit and reflect
On the goodness and love I so often reject

Make me whole again Father, in you do I trust
Cuz I'm faced with a road I know is a must
From deep within my soul cries
As you mend all the pieces and forgive my failed tries
From deep within my soul cries
Through the pain and the tears I shall arise
From deep within my soul cries
A transparent story's where my power **lies**
Not my hips n' not my thighs… but the truth in my eyes
From deep within my souls cries
Another chance at life
Another phoenix flies…

Support Your Local Small Businesses:

"I am so grateful for the experience to work with Tanicia 'Shamay Speaks' Currie on the Breaking Through Barriers book project. She's such an amazing leader, coach and friend. More importantly, Tanicia always go over and above to make sure her client's needs are met 1000%! Thank you again Tanicia, you've made my first book project experience one of lifetime." Kanishia Wallace

"It was great working with Tanicia. She helped me every step of the way during the process of becoming an author; from compartmentalizing my ideas and getting them on paper to marketing my book and getting my first customer." Rachel Edwards

"Shamay has been a joy to work with. From the first time i met her she was very encouraging and pleasant and very clear on the vision and what she expected of me. She was very professional and is a woman of her word. If she says she is going to do something she does it. She was excellent when it came to meeting deadlines and often met them earlier than promised.

Shamay provided a welcoming atmosphere in all of our workshops and provided great resources and snacks (smile). She made herself available in a way that showed her passion for not only her vision but our vision and goals. I definitely trust her to publish my next project and will be reaching out to her."

Thank you Shamay! Love, Monique

Since July 2016, Shamay has been the creative visionary and publisher for these amazing and powerful book compilations:

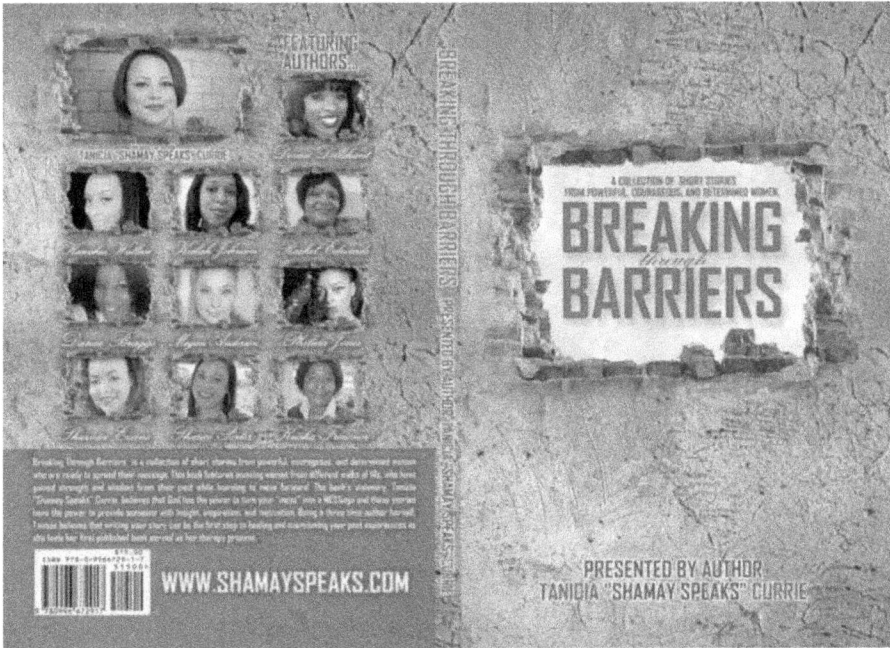

Released July 9th, 2016

July 9th, 2016 I had an extremely blessed weekend. It really had my spirit full. I appreciate all the awesome words the ladies said about me, made me tear up. Everything meant so much to me. My deepest gratitude to every amazing woman who allowed me to assist them in becoming authors.

#BreakingBarriers #Testimonies #Authors #MakeItHappen #SkyisTheLimit #ShamaySpeaks Www.shamayspeaks.com

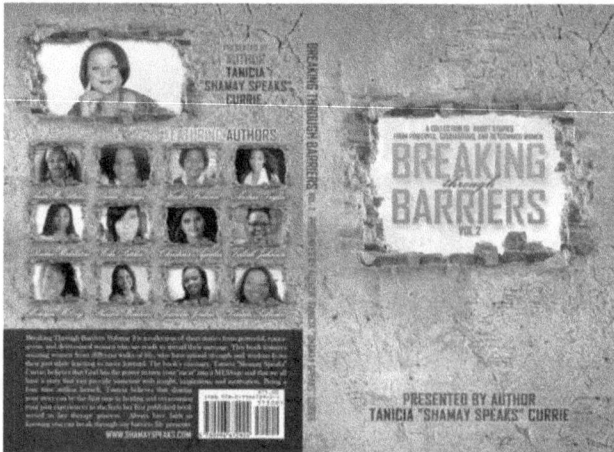

Released January 7th, 2017

January 7th, 2017 I had such a blessed day; words cannot express how I feel. Helping others succeed and be able to bless others. I may provide opportunities but these beautiful women give me the opportunity to assist and guide while walking in purpose. Thank you ladies, for choosing me to work with. It's an honor, congratulations! This is just the beginning♥♥ I'm very proud of each of you continue to step out on faith. Love you y'all! Special thanks to everyone who attended...It humbles me so much the whole experience. It's much more than business, it's about changing lives, providing healing, and stepping out on faith to accomplish goals and dreams. Now I really understand what it means when God said esteem others higher than yourself. Shout out and thanks to my amazing friend and business partner Shauny B Smith for the awesome book cover and my phenomenal cousin for the editing Ilesha Coco Graham and Supreme Photography Marcus Wright. Beautiful and perfect song by Taliah Johnson and Ben Rivera. #Blessed #Thankful #Grateful #AssistingOtherAmazingPeople I would love to work with more amazing women, if you want to come become an author in 2017 contact me text your email address to 925-421-0221

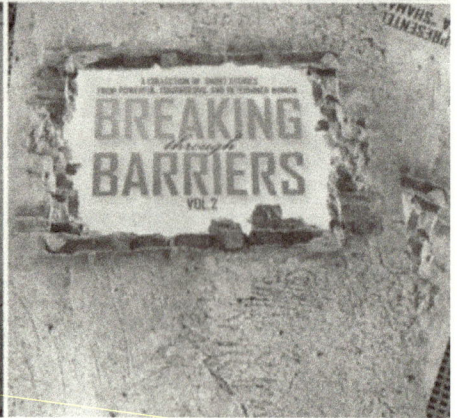

Broken Into Brilliance Volume 1

(Released June 17th, 2017)

Congrats to these beautiful women. I am so honored to have worked with you all. I look forward to your individual book launches. You all make the world proud and will change lives. Thank you for choosing me to lead and guide you. I am beyond blessed ♥♥♥. May God continue to lay put your path of success 👍👍👍.

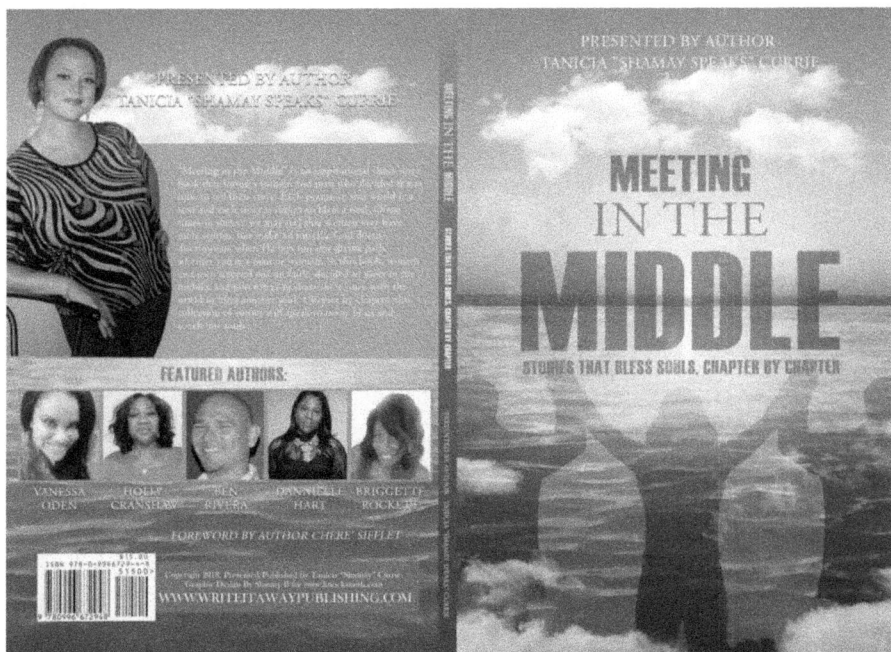
On January 13th, 2018, I launched my 5th book in a little over 2 years. These 5 awesome authors choose to work with me even knowing I was having major surgery, which shows genuine love. I appreciate every one of you and I feel blessed that you choose me to assist you. Congratulations, thank you for being genuine, open, nonjudgmental, and transparent. Your stories bless others chapter by chapter. I was finally to bring men and women together to inspire the world. Y'all are all amazing, I look forward to your solo books.

Thank you to our amazing keynote speaker who did her thang @moeministry you're headed to bigger stages. Your message is powerful. I can't wait to wear my shirt. #GetOverYourself

Thank you to Tim and Ben for their touching worship songs 🎵 🎙 🎤

Thank you Chere' for blessing the book 💜 💜

Thank you to those who always got my back Shaun @knocksmithmusic Danae @danae_all_day

Marcus @supreme_photography_77

My sister Marie.

Love you all, let takeover 2018 👌 👌 👌 💜 💜 💜 🙏 🙏 💜 💜

Live your dreams, anything is possible!

9Quota (925) Art and Music Awards where we give recognition to various artists who contribute greatly to the art, fashion, design and music community. This compilation of talented individuals represent the rich culture of our community and shine light on the up and comers in the area. With the support of the community nominating and voting for these people they get a chance to be inspired as well as inspire others. We have been featured on BET, MTV, Vh1, the Contra Costa Times, East County Times, Mercury News, Oakland Tribune, 89.5 FM Ozcat Radio, and 106.1 KMEL. We are well respected by city officials and always comply with the wishes of the community as well as the Pittsburg Police Department.

This event is completed organized and funded by the 9Quota staff. We take pride in our unique approach in contributing to art in the community. We are fortunate enough to present this event in the historic California Theatre located in the beautiful new revived Downtown Pittsburg area. Previously we have held this event is the Lesher Center for arts in Walnut Creek California and also other locations in Brentwood and Concord. Each winner is presented with a trophy with their named engraved on it to personalize the achievement. We thank all of our supporters.

Branches of Community Services

Tanicia Currie – CEO
Founder- Betty Conner
E-mail: communitybranches925@gmail.com
www.branchesofcommunityservices.org
Business Line: (925) 709-4406
Tax ID #- Available upon request

Our Mission:

Our mission is to support the community by providing branches of educational support, resources, and opportunities for personal development. In fulfilling our mission, we hope to encourage the community to create a cycle of giving back to spread a message of universal community empowerment.

Special thanks to our dedicated team:

Danae Braggs, Shauny B Smith, Miranda O' Hare, Marcus Wright, and all of our supportive and loyal sponsors!

It is no surprise that much of today's media has migrated to online platforms, but there are few truly innovative visionaries who recognize that print, images, videos and music are rapidly converging. One of these leaders is Knocksmith Magazine which is bringing all of these mediums and their fans together to experience something profoundly new and unique.

Knocksmith Magazine offers a physical print magazine that is integrated with online music and video services, via QR apps, codes and giveaways. The production team behind Knocksmith Magazine has showcased some of the emerging superstars of the independent hip-hop scene. The insightful interviews are presented as videos that are accompanied by written articles and full page images. This rich, interactive media offers a 360 degree view of the artist that can't be found anywhere else in the music industry. In addition to intimate looks at rising musical artists, Knocksmith Magazine is also the platform of choice for fans to explore the music scene. The exhaustive collection of artists and music found on the Knocksmith Magazine catalogue enables fans to hear new songs, link to download sites and find similar artists. Finally, Knocksmith Magazine is a proud supporter of music lovers. Through their "Save the Record Stores" campaign, the magazine is helping to preserve an important but endangered part of the music industry. That is why Knocksmith Magazine encourages purchase of music both online and through neighborhood record stores.

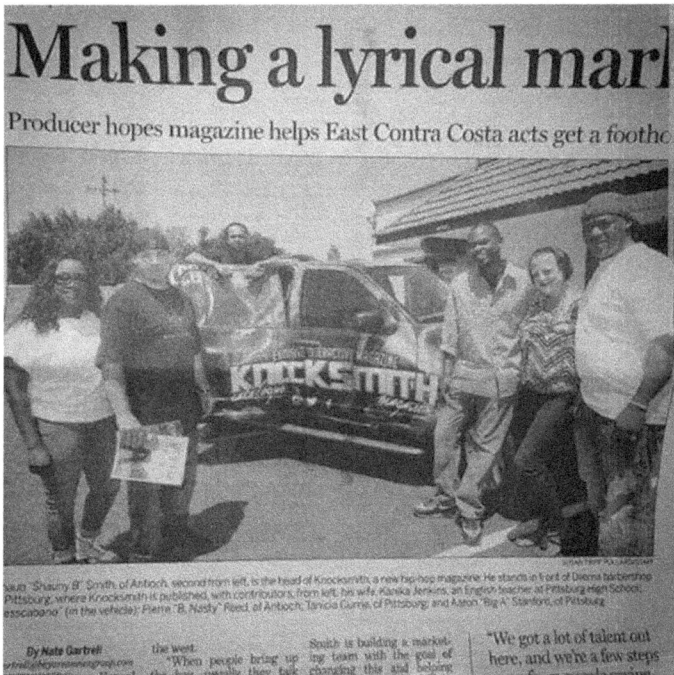

Making a lyrical mark

Producer hopes magazine helps East Contra Costa acts get a foothold

Need an award-winning great designer for book covers and/or graphic design work:

Contact Shauny B Smith with KnockSmith Magazine:

www.KnocksmithMazagine.com

172

173

Live life, don't let it live you!~ Anonymous

Thank you for supporting this book and the amazing women featured ☺

www.ingramcontent.com/pod-product-compliance
Lightning Source LLC
Chambersburg PA
CBHW020857090426
42736CB00008B/408